K-9 Bodyguards

TS-233

Publisher's Note:

The methods and training philosophies put forth in this text have been tested and applied by author Mike Harlow, a professional guard-dog trainer and an experienced K-9 officer. The publisher wishes to emphasize, however, that these teachings are not necessarily recommended by T.F.H. Publications, Inc., and the publisher cannot assume responsibility for any damages or injuries that may be directly or indirectly related to the applications of the training methods contained herein.

Additionally, these methods and teaching devices are not for everyone: training dogs in bitework is inherently dangerous, and reasonable safety is always advised.

The author cannot make or imply any guarantee for the lawful applications or usage of a dog. This responsibility rests squarely on the shoulders of the dog's owner and/handler.

Trainers should exercise extreme caution when working with a dog and should never do so in the presence of children or in public places. Precautionary measures should always be considered for the safety of the trainers, the dogs, and others.

Overleaf: American Pit Bull Terrier "Blue Billy" of Watchdog Kennels. **Title Page:** American Bulldog "Patch" owned by Mike Harlow and bred by Bodyguard Kennels.

© 1995 by T.F.H. Publications, Inc.

Distributed in the UNITED STATES to the Pet Trade by T.F.H. Publications, Inc., One T.F.H. Plaza, Neptune City, NJ 07753; distributed in the UNITED STATES to the Bookstore and Library Trade by National Book Network, Inc. 4720 Boston Way, Lanham MD 20706; in CANADA to the Pet Trade by H & L Pet Supplies Inc., 27 Kingston Crescent, Kitchener, Ontario N2B 2T6; Rolf C. Hagen Ltd., 3225 Sartelon Street, Montreal 382 Quebec; in CANADA to the Book Trade by Vanwell Publishing Ltd., 1 Northrup Crescent, St. Catharines, Ontario L2M 6P5 ; in ENGLAND by T.F.H. Publications, PO Box 15, Waterlooville PO7 6BQ; in AUSTRALIA AND THE SOUTH PACIFIC by T.F.H. (Australia), Pty. Ltd., Box 149, Brookvale 2100 N.S.W., Australia; in NEW ZEALAND by Brooklands Aquarium Ltd. 5 McGiven Drive, New Plymouth, RD1 New Zealand; in Japan by T.F.H. Publications, Japan—Jiro Tsuda, 10-12-3 Ohjidai, Sakura, Chiba 285, Japan; in SOUTH AFRICA by Lopis (Pty) Ltd., P.O. Box 39127, Booysens, 2016, Johannesburg, South Africa. Published by T.F.H. Publications, Inc.
MANUFACTURED IN THE UNITED STATES OF AMERICA
BY T.F.H. PUBLICATIONS, INC.

K-9 Bodyguards

by Mike Harlow

Dedication

This book is dedicated to the memory of my good friend, Deputy Jim Dickinson, who was murdered in the line of duty in 1989 in Palm Beach County, Florida. Jim was 29.

Acknowledgments

When I first set out to write this book, I had no idea how much help I would need, and how much I actually got came as a shock. It kind of restored my dwindling faith in human nature. Photos and training input came from every corner of the country.

In no particular order I would like to thank the following people without whose help, this book might not have attained this size and quality. Bob Anderson; Ron Shunk; Doug Madigan; Al Banuelos; Norm Garner; Lance Jackson (who wears a scar from my dog); John D. Johnson; John Blackwell; Kyle Symmes; Pete Curley; Gonnie Schaffer; Larry Koura of RodeHawg Kennels; Steve LeClerc; Tom Morris; James Booth; Charles Warnic; Ken Buzzell; Steve Baccari; Casey Couturier; Mrs. Andrews; Al Batchelor; Illini Kennels.

Special thanks to Mark Evans, who did the decoy work in the river just for this book; and to my telephone companion, pen pal, Bulldog Guru and all around nice lady, Karen Koura, who is totally to blame for this book's very existence. I was just minding my own business one day when she said, "Hey, why don't you write a book?" To author Jerry Yulsman, who told me "Today, only James Joyce or Hemingway would get a handwritten manuscript past a publisher's wastebasket!" To my mom and dad for never giving up on me in spite of my best efforts. To the gal with whom I've shared a bedroom for the last four years, whose shapely form shamelessly graces many of the pages of this book—Patch is a bitch but I love her anyway.

Finally, to my training assistant, equipment inspector, famous dog wrestler, toy tester, ice cream taster, dinosaur collector, cartoon critic and all around best buddy, my son Brent.

Contents

About the Author

Mike Harlow was born in Chicago in 1948. While he was still quite young, the family moved to Levittown, Pennsylvania where he grew up. During this time, a few stray dogs followed him home but didn't stay very long. The family always had cats. Convincing his mom of the importance of a dog for a growing boy seemed an exercise in futility.

Little League baseball, wrestling, gymnastics, water polo, archery and a girl named Jennie kept him off the streets and out of trouble until 1969, when he enlisted in the U.S. Navy. Before earning his gold wings as an air crewman he was to undergo much schooling in jet engine repair, hand-to-hand combat, swimming, first aid, survival schools in both California and the Philippines and more. Mike wound up in a combat rescue helicopter squadron in the Philippines that rotated back and forth to Vietnam for two-and-a-half years. They were known as the "Big Mothers" and their job was rescuing downed aviators at sea and over land. The "Big Mother" crew was the only helicopter crew to ever win the Congressional Medal of Honor in any war. Mike has two rescues to his credit. While in the Philippines, he came across something very rare indeed, a stray dog. He immediately took it in and entrusted it to the care of

The author with bad company.

his roommate in Olongapo City. Mike's services were requested in the Gulf of Tonkin and he was off again. When he returned 60 days later, he learned that the neighbors had noticed his dog in the yard, and it had become the main course at their barbecue. Even the Vietnamese kept dogs as pets and valued them as sentinels. U.S. Navy SEALS used silenced pistols to quiet these canine sentinels. They were referred to as "hush puppies."

Mike returned home with both medals and many memories in 1973. He went to work as a police officer in Connecticut. It wasn't quite as rewarding as rescuing P.O.W.'s, but it was nearly as much fun and addictive. He'd found a home. About 11 years later he was in a small town in Florida fighting crime. He noticed an old friend was making a sizable dent in the crime rate in a neighboring town with the aid of a dog. Now an avid dog enthusiast, Mike rode as an observer for a couple of nights and witnessed the awesome effectiveness of a trained police dog. That did it. In short order, a demo was given for the town council and Mike got the okay to start training his personal dog, a Rottweiler named Zack (named after a renowned knifemaker and personal friend). Because of dental problems, Zack was washed out and replaced with a German Shepherd who would soon gain fame as "Sick Nick." Much of Mike's training and street K-9 application was learned with Nick. He credits the dog with saving his life on more than one

occasion as well as the lives of other officers. Perhaps this book will give Nick some of the credit he deserves. He wasn't "Rin Tin Tin," just an average dog, yet he did miraculous things on a regular basis. After having owned such a dog, Mike plans to never be without a trained dog again.

Leathercrafting is Mike's main hobby. Holsters, belts, knife sheaths, harnesses, leashes and fancy collars are his favorite projects. Only the customer's bank account will limit the degree of ornamentation available on his museum-quality collars. Snake, lizard, shark, elephant, ostrich and alligator are some of the exotic hides available to the discriminating owners of worthy dogs. His motto is, "The finest dogs deserve the finest collars."

Mike likes dogs and has serious doubts about anyone who doesn't. He plans to train them professionally as soon as he has the space. With 16 years as a policeman and K-9 officer, he should be well qualified to become a professional dog trainer. He is currently spearheading a movement to get the American Bulldog accepted as a bonafide police dog. As well as authoring this book, he has written occasional articles for the *National Bulldogger Magazine.*

One of his favorite Merle Haggard songs contains the following lyrics:

There's good guys and outlaws
And right guys and southpaws
There's good dogs and all kinds
of cats.

Purpose

This book's life began as a training record for my German Shepherd police dog. He and I were employed full time as a police K-9 unit in a small farming town in South Florida. I thought it would be a good idea to have something that could be shown to a jury who might have to make a decision as to whether my dog's training was adequate, and to repudiate any claim by a plaintiff's council that the dog was trained in nothing but the most professional methods.

This training record would come in handy for future K-9 handlers that I planned to train. It was and is a tough town and needed more than one dog patrolling its streets. The town had all the crime that goes along with a teeming drug trade.

When I made up my mind to make this manual into a complete book, I decided to aim it primarily at the novice; although experts should also be able to learn a thing or two. I'm still learning about dogs and their training, and I don't want the reader to think

Opposite: The American Bulldog is an excellent choice for K-9 police training. **Below:** "Sick Nick," an outstanding police dog and the prime motivation for this book.

I'm offering this up as the Holy Grail of dog training. I only offer it as a collection of methods that I have personal experience with or have observed being used by professional trainers, and I can guarantee that they are effective. The methods contained herein are not based on theory. They are not something related to sport. They are meant to work on the street and I'm here to tell you that the street is far different than the competition field. It is almost impossible to get killed on the competition field. It is incredibly easy to get killed on the street. The fact that these methods have been tested on the street is the essence of what makes this book different from all other dog-training books. Some of these methods saved my life. Others, however, endangered my life and I will tell you which ones.

One of my goals in writing this book is to provide the novice with a reference on how to train a dog for police work or personal protection. If the civilian thinks it leans toward the police end of the spectrum, remember that it all crosses over to the private sector as well.

So, you think you have little need for a dog trained to track men? You may not have a need to track any killers, but when your two-year-old daughter wanders away from the picnic table and into the national forest, your trained tracking dog can locate her more quickly than you can locate a phone to dial 911.

You might enjoy it so much that you might want to join a search and rescue organization. Tracking is a lot of fun and easy to learn. So is every other phase in this book.

Schutzhund and Ringsport aren't covered in this book because they are sports and don't apply to the real world as well as they could. I also have no experience in those areas and have no business writing about them. Hopefully many of these methods will carry over and help the people who enjoy these sports.

Whether you're a police officer or a civilian, there is a pride of ownership that is unequaled after your dog has completed this training. If you or your significant other wants to jog in Central Park at three in the morning, you may do so secure in the knowledge that you will jog unmolested. A dog trained by the simple methods contained in this book can provide peace of mind that no electronic alarm can. An alarm can only tell you that you have just become a victim. The trained dog can warn of the presence of an intruder, can announce entry and then can rid your domicile of the unwanted vermin.

You say you have no use for a riot-trained dog? Well, a young couple walking on a South Florida beach recently could have used one. It was well after dark when their romantic moonlight walk turned to tragedy. A gang of youths swarmed them and the man was savagely beaten and robbed while six teenage boys took turns raping the woman. A protection-trained dog could

Tracking is an easily trained skill and practical for any and all dog owners. Your dog's keen sense of smell can be used to find lost jewelry, wallet, child—just about anything.

have handled five times that number with ease.

Ask any owner of a formidable dog what the average reaction is as he walks his dog toward a group of young toughs late at night. They will always give you and your dog the entire sidewalk, and more often than not they will relinquish the entire side of the street to you. So, please don't tell me that dogs don't deter crime.

I'm always astonished at the number of people who are alarmed at our escalating burglary rate due to the influx of drugs into this country. Many of them seek my advice on how to increase their safety. I usually tell them to buy a gun and learn how

to use it. It requires less maintenance and is less of an intrusion into their spare time. The usual response is "I hate guns" or "I couldn't shoot anyone." The next answer is get a formidable dog. They are a wonderful alternative to guns and are not only a terrific deterrent, they are great company as well. They are the ideal companion for those night deposits at the bank or the A.T.M. (a growing favorite for muggers).

For the civilian, the purpose of this book is to provide you with a companion whose presence, training and loyalty will give you a feeling of security and peace of mind that a gun can't equal and a burglar alarm can't compete with. A dog's friendship and loyalty are unquestionable, his value incalculable.

Police officers, there will come a time, if it hasn't already, when you roll up on something in progress like a domestic assault, and the husband is 12 feet tall and doesn't like people in uniforms. Do you rush in and possibly get disarmed and killed, or do you wait for backup and watch him kill his wife in the meantime? If you're a K-9 cop, your backup is already there, and dogs have a decided advantage when it comes to getting the attention of someone who is not a

Schutzhund and Ringsport are two sports that are fun to compete in, however, the skills involved are fairly useless in real-life situations. The training methods in this book have been tested on the street and proven to be effective.

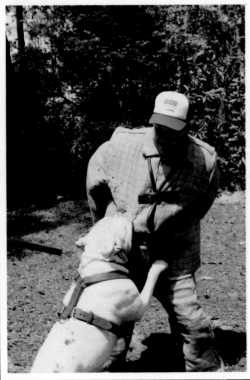

good listener. Most arguments and fights stop immediately at the mere arrival of a K-9 unit. Hank Williams, Jr., is aware of it and even wrote a song about it called "Attitude Adjustment." It has some of the funniest lyrics I've ever heard and remains a favorite of K-9 officers everywhere.

For police, the purpose of this book is to provide you with a new tool that will enable you to hear and smell things in the dark in much the same manner as a flashlight lets you see in the dark. This enables officers to find things in the dark that they were previously unable to find and hold criminals that they were previously unable to catch.

At no time in recent history has a law-enforcement agency had an unlimited budget, and probably never will. Many crowd situations develop that require several officers to maintain control. Additional officers cost money. Dogs require no salary and a modest upkeep. The K-9 provides instant backup and can move more people than a 20-man riot squad. The versatility of your department will be expanded because of the dog's ability to find criminals, evidence, lost articles, children, old folks, narcotics and bombs, not to mention its ability for crowd control and officer protection.

My ultimate purpose for both police and private citizens is to provide them with an alternative to a shooting situation. I believe this book and your hard work will combine to produce a dog that you will cherish for years to come.

For the civilian who thinks he doesn't need all that this book covers, yet still wants a real protection dog, do not skip the socialization or the obedience sections. To do so would possibly create a dog that is unaware that 98 percent of the people he meets are good people and not deserving of his special skills. He would also be uncontrollable and impossible to call off once he has stopped the aggressor. You don't want him to kill anyone.

You could stop after completing "socialization" and "obedience" and have a wonderful dog, but although he would be a good deterrent, he could not be counted on to do the right thing in a dangerous situation. Some formidable breeds have gotten themselves into big trouble over the years by reacting to a situation in a manner that scares the general population out of its wits, with the help of the media's sensationalistic reports of vicious dogs attacking innocent humans. Pit Bulls are the current scapegoats but are followed closely by Rottweilers. If you know that your dog has a propensity to eventually bite someone because of a strong protective drive and a lack of fear of humans, don't panic! This does *not* mean he's vicious. If he bites you and your family members without provocation or just to assert his dominance, he is not worth the price of his chow. But if he is only showing a potential of biting but loves his family, he is a valuable animal and should be trained as soon as possible so that his

Dog or Gun? If you need protection, the choice is yours, but in the author's opinion, a well-trained protection dog is a top-notch alternative to buying a gun, if you have the time and patience for training. Remember, a bullet cannot be called back once you've pulled the trigger. **Above & Below:** Would you mess with either of these two dogs?.

abilities are channeled in the right direction. Protection training as taught in this book programs him to bite *only* aggressive types.

This doesn't mean you'll be able to let him roam the neighborhood. Someone could attempt to shoo him out of their yard with a fly swatter and wind up in the hospital. I believe most Pit Bull incidents happen this way, or else sense must be employed to prevent it. Most other protection breeds will also fight because the same thing that makes Pit Bulls fight is also present in the other breeds. It is sometimes referred to as hardness or toughness or even gameness, but it is just a desire to dominate each other and is very pronounced in the Pit Bull. American Bulldogs are similar in

Rode Hawg Kennels "Perdi," a purebred American Bulldog.

by owners just keeping their dogs on chains where people can walk up to them. The dogs are normally the most people-friendly dogs in the world, but they have strong prey drives as well as protection drives. In the wrong hands, they can create disaster. In the right home, the Pit Bull is one of the best dogs ever conceived. I speak from experience. I've owned three American Pit Bull Terriers, and never had a single bad incident. The dogs will fight and common temperament, although not to the extent that Pit Bulls are. The American Bulldog is a much more tractable fellow around other dogs. I still wouldn't let him roam, but he is a bit more relaxed.

So, if "socialization" and "obedience" is the only training you give your dog, you will be rewarded with a dog who will be a well-behaved companion to be proud of. Don't be surprised when strangers compliment his good manners.

Above: The American Bulldog shares many favorable characteristics with his close cousin, the APBT, but is much larger in size. **Below:** Two American Bulldogs, Spanky and Kink, owned by Sue Miller.

Breed Suitability

The APBT is an athletic, tough dog well suited for K-9 protection. This gorgeous dog, "Whiskey," lives with a pretty mistress. It's doubtful that second story men will try *this* balcony.

There are preconceived notions on any subject and everyone has an opinion as to what is the best dog for protection work. Some of the opinions are based on knowledge and experience, but others are based on sentimentality, ignorance and worst of all, tradition. Collies would probably get the vote of the sentimentalists due to all of the wonderful exploits of "Lassie." The ignorant group would probably go with Great Danes and St. Bernards, thinking that bigger is better. Sometimes it is, but not in the case of working dogs. A working dog will be defined as a dog capable of doing police work, Schutzhund, Ringsport or personal protection. Agility is a requirement of a working dog, which leaves out all of the giant breeds. Traditionalists will tell you that the German Shepherd is the best dog because most police dogs are Shepherds. Remember, just a few centuries ago it was considered proper etiquette to throw the contents of a chamber pot (toilet) out the window of a second-story building as long as you yelled the warning "Alley oop!" before the toss. It was traditional, therefore, acceptable. Fortunately we developed better technology. Let's not let tradition lead us around by the nose. The German Shepherd is a fine animal and scores high in the all-around dog category when his temperament is right. But getting the right temperament can be outrageously expensive because one must go to Europe to obtain good specimens. Dobermans are nearly extinct in police circles because of unsuitable temperaments. Rottweilers are great as well but are difficult to train because they are stubborn and slow to mature. And just like Shepherds, they are expensive to get.

There are two American breeds that are suitable, locally available, sound, strong, hard as nails and sell for a fraction of what other breeds command. Because of ignorance and tradition these two breeds have until very recently been categorized as being unsuitable for the task. This was because of their historical background and the fact that no one had ever tried them as working dogs. Now they *are* being trained and they are doing extremely well.

The breeds of which I speak are close relatives, namely the American Bulldog and the American Pit Bull Terrier (which is basically the same dog with about 12 to 15 percent terrier blood added for speed and agility). The American Bulldog (AB) is actually the original

English Bulldog from 200 years ago. The current English Bulldog is the result of people breeding for type instead of performance. The English dogs were imported into the U.S. in their original form. While the British bred their dogs down in size, bulldogs in this country were bred in the original form because the early settlers needed tough dogs for predator control, as catch dogs and for family guards. They quietly survived in isolated pockets in the southeastern United States, where they are still used for the same purposes. The breed has just been discovered by the Schutzhund crowd and there are very few American Bulldogs with a Schutzhund II title. The first such title holder is named

A good working dog, and one suitable for personal protection, should be agile, durable, and temperamentally sound. Great size is a plus but not a necessity.

"Predator" and he is owned and trained by Al Banuelos of Los Angeles, California. The name of Al's kennel is Jaws of Stone. Presently, training is in progress on a Predator son named Ike. He apparently has his father's drive. A daughter of the same famous dog, Lulu, was the winner of the 1990 "Iron Dog Triathalon," which consists of a tug-of-war, an agility course and a weight pull. Lulu is owned and trained by Mark Landers of Elizabeth, Colorado, owner of Mountain Gator Kennels. Several other ABs are being trained at this time and it won't surprise me in the slightest to see many more Schutzhund titles among them.

The American Pit Bull Terrier (APBT) has already won many Schutzhund titles, as he is a fairly popular dog and well established. The APBTs go about 50 to 70 pounds on the average and ABs go about 85 to 120 pounds. Everything that made these two breeds known for their unsavory past job descriptions makes them terrific as working dogs. The qualities to which I refer are ability, brains, determination, willingness to please, strength and courage. Shepherds and Rottweilers are very good dogs. Our two American breeds are great dogs. Since they haven't yet been discovered by the show crowd they aren't neurotic bedwetters, but stable, self-assured, sound and courageous dogs that can handle the stress and the intense training involved in this demanding line of work. They deserve a closer look.

Yes, there are other breeds considered suitable for the task but one, the Belgian Malinois, is rather small in my opinion, though amply possessed of grit and determination. According to all reports he is as hard as nails but a dog so lightly constructed can be overpowered, picked up and thrown into the nearest dumpster. If I'm going to tell anyone to stand behind a 60-pound dog, I'll be talking about a Pit Bull. I've seen them bring 2,000-pound Brahma bulls down singlehanded, and I'm aware of a 55-pound dog in Alaska that held a 900-pound moose that tried to charge its owner. The dog was on a chain at the time.

A famous trainer whose credentials run off the page once

said that "you could have one considerably smaller than the 60 pound standard and still have all the dog you would ever need." That trainer was none other than the late Bill Koehler. When Bill spoke, other trainers listened. Another famous dog trainer, Captain Arthur Haggerty, is reportedly focusing

my life that I don't feel a need to fill in the spare time grooming a long-haired dog. All that hair picks up all manner of vegetation if you live in a country setting as I do. It also requires clipping from time to time.

The only other dog that is up to the task is the German

The great size and agility of the American Bulldog are traits which have finally been discovered by those invovled in Schutzhund competition. Notice the lean lines and musculature of this well proportioned AB.

his interest solely on the APBT nowadays. Haggerty has been in the business practically forever and he knows what works in protection.

There are no less than three other breeds from Belgium worth mentioning: the Bouvier des Flandres, the Tervuren and the Belgian Sheepdog. The Bouvier is my pick of the three because of its size and power. The other two are reportedly good dogs but suffer the same disadvantage as the Malinois. Worse still is their long hair. I have enough to do in

version of the Bouvier, known as the Giant Schnauzer. He isn't a true giant breed, just the largest of the schnauzers. I'm told by knowledgeable people that he is a fine animal. He is used in Germany with success. If someone would groom him for me I'd like to own one someday. In a city environment any of these dogs would be just fine, especially if you think hours of grooming is fun. These dogs all have the right stuff and that's all that counts. They will all get the job done.

If all the foregoing wasn't sufficient in explaining my choice of the AB over the traditional German Shepherd for protection or police work, then perhaps the following will clear up any confusion:

a fighting dog?,' screw up your eyes to recreate that same suspicious look and answer, 'And why do you want a dog that will bring you sheep?' Thanks Carl, for a good book and a good answer.

The German Shepherd Dog is the traditional image of a police dog, however, it is very difficult to find one with suitable temperament for training without going overseas.

1. I love German Shepherds. They are really good dogs, though costly.

2. I love Rottweilers more because they're tougher and have a more intimidating appearance. Never underestimate intimidation value. They're tough to train, stubborn and costly.

3. Bulldogs are more intimidating, tougher and more durable than Rottweilers. They are easily trained, reasonably priced and made in America.

Dr. Carl Semencic may have summed it up better than I ever could on the last page of his book *The World of Fighting Dogs* (T.F.H. Publications) when he said, "The first time someone walks up to you with his German Shepherd with that unfriendly, suspicious gleam in his eye and pops the question 'Why do you want to own

Don't get me wrong. I like most dogs, especially Norwich and Jack Russell Terriers, but I prefer a multi-purpose dog if possible. Any of them can be your companion, but I also want my companion to be alert and protective—big enough to be a deterrent, tough enough to be a real thug buster and durable enough that if he has to go in harm's way, he will not only survive, but prevail. Few dogs will meet that criteria. That's why I choose a dog from the working group. They have this versatility.

My personal preference of dog to protect me in a bad neighborhood is the American Bulldog. His physical abilities place him so far ahead of the competition that it really isn't a competition at all. He can track at least as well as a German

Shepherd. His short coat is easily cared for and needs no grooming or trimming. He has enough body weight that it is unlikely that he will be picked up and thrown. As with the Pit Bull, he'll never be slung off. If someone can somehow ignore the bite pressure and land a solid punch on him, it's not unlikely that he'll wag his tail and show a marked increase in his enthusiasm. Remember, combat is his reason for being. It is his area of expertise. To say it is unnecessary to teach him the hard bite would be an understatement. He is the quintessential gladiator of the canine race. In working dog terms, he is state of the art.

I think the use of Bulldogs in police work is overdue and I plan to do whatever I can to make it happen.

Another breed that could shine would be the Bullmastiff. He is big enough and powerful enough to stop whatever or whoever is in his way. He is very reasonably priced and is in good supply. Because of his size, I think he would have limitations as far as hurdles and long tracks and he wouldn't last long in summer heat. For these reasons, I'd like to see the breeders start breeding the smaller ones that would have the stamina necessary for this tough job. As a personal and home guardian, I don't think you could do much better. Living in South Florida, I would have no use for him. Summer is about seven months long here and a working Bullmastiff would suffer. So why does this dog interest me at all?

Because he has a characteristic that is virtually unique among the suitable protection breeds.

His reason for being is to run down, catch and hold poachers without mauling them. I thought it was typical breed hype until I met Blackjack. He was an AKC (American Kennel Club) Champion and was fully protection trained. I was asked to do some on-lead agitation by his owner. I was unable to extract so much as a "wuff" out of him as I closed on him. He just sat quietly and waited until I was close enough, then nailed me and sat down with the padded sleeve in his mouth. No shaking. No growling. When I tried to wrench the sleeve out of his jaws, it became painfully obvious that I was going nowhere until he or his

The Rottweiler is a formidable, intimidating breed whose mere looks are enough to frighten most human beings. However, these dogs are difficult to train and very expensive.

master said so. Running apprehension was excellent. He easily closed the gap and took the sleeve. Then he put the brakes on and stopped me even though I was trying to drag him down the field with me. Again, no shaking or growling. He just held me until the handler arrived and outed him (made him release). It was almost

requested. A married couple had gone out to dinner. Shortly after their departure, the door glass broke and a hand came through to twist the inside knob. When it did, the pet Bullmastiff seized the hand, sat down and quietly waited several hours for the return of his family. When they returned, they called the police. The man's hand

The Bullmastiff is a large, powerful dog with a gentle disposition, making it a good choice as a personal protection dog. Photo courtesy of Ada Braun.

as though the dog was being careful not to hurt me so he could play with me some more. A smaller female was then brought out and gave a duplicate performance. I don't think either dog barked during the entire exercise. I was notably impressed.

A breeder sent me a reprinted newspaper story from Thailand with a brochure that I'd

was not damaged. I believe the Bullmastiff has the power to remove an arm if he so desires, yet they are gentle as long as the situation doesn't escalate.

There are of course many other breeds claiming to be good guards. Some are and some aren't. Among those that are is the Neopolitan Mastiff, but I wouldn't have one of these in my house. I consider the amount of drooling to be unacceptable.

The Old English Mastiff is arguably the oldest purebred dog breed known to exist. It is what most guard dogs in the world descended from. The Mastiffs of old were very fierce and needed very little provocation before going into action. They were always very large dogs and were known for their courage and power. That was then. Today they are perhaps a little larger if anything, but the legendary fierceness is supposed to have subsided to a considerable degree. I've read and heard from knowledgeable people, including professional trainers, that they are 200-pound throw rugs. Not being a dog-show enthusiast, I have seen very few of these dogs indeed. I have never known any trainers who were actually able to get a rise out of one.

I recently was called about an ad I placed in *Dog World* magazine. The caller was Tom Bland from the central Florida area, not far from me. He owned an American Bulldog, Preacher, and wanted me to train the dog. We arrived at a mutually acceptable agreement so that I could start training the dog. I visited Tom's home and started the dog's training program. During one of the breaks, Tom wanted to find out if his Mastiff would actually bite if a suitable moment presented itself. Armed with the limited knowledge above, I smiled. I instructed Tom to put Preacher away and bring in the 200-pound couch potato to face the inevitable shame and

The Bouvier des Flandres is a big dog with a long history as a working breed. His inherent guarding ability, strength, and size make him an ideal protector.

degradation of watching this giant dog cower. Wolf was put on the agitation cable and was very happy to join us in the training area. He was attempting to play with Tom as I began my sneaky approach. I was doing an Academy Award performance but Wolf couldn't have cared less. He was ecstatic to be with his dad and was really intent on ignoring me. I finally started hurling disparaging remarks about his lineage at the top of my lungs and charged. Wolf realized this was serious. His tail stopped wagging, the ground shook slightly with his low rumble of a growl and he closed his huge jaws on the nearest part of my anatomy. I was wearing a soft sleeve suitable for advanced dogs with a padded leather gauntlet under it. This turned out to be a smart move. Even with all this padding, I felt his two upper canines on top of my forearm. They didn't penetrate, but they did hurt. This was his first bite and it was an awesome one. The second one was every bit as awesome.

Now that I have this under my belt, I still don't fancy myself an expert on Mastiffs, but I certainly have a new respect for them.

I keep hearing that Airedales are supposed to be good, but I have yet to see one I would take as a gift. I've never even seen one used as a police dog. Before I can recommend this dog, I'll need to see some good working examples. Most of the aforementioned breeds are dogs with which I have personal experience. As you may have noticed, I lean heavily toward the fighting breeds, because what makes a good fighter makes a good protector. There is another dog in this category worth mentioning, the Presa Canario or just Canary Dog.

He gets his name not from the little yellow bird but from his geographic origin, the Canary Islands. This dog looks very much like a giant Pit Bull and his main purpose until just recently has been that of a fighter and a catch dog extraordinaire. They go

The Giant Schnauzer, a breed similar to the Bouvier des Flandres, has been used extensively in Germany as a protection and police dog.

The Neapolitan Mastiff is a large dog and a staunch defender of home and property. In the foreground is "Mosa," a 150-pound blue female, and in the background is Ch. Sultan.

between 100 and 130 pounds but are reported to have agility and speed rivaling Pit Bulls. If this is true, we may be looking at the replacement for the top five breeds considered suitable for protection and police work. He is quite expensive. For 15 years I've only heard one recurring complaint from Pit Bull lovers, that they wish their dogs were bigger. Well? I might try a Canary Dog myself. If they're half as good as they look, they should be formidable and capable.

Presently, I'm seeing several Malinois being trained. One trainer tells me they're high strung and require a lot of "maintenance." He means they sometimes forget that they're supposed to out on command and their attitude needs frequent adjustments. The same is true in the recall exercise. At times a running man is just too much to resist and away they go. On the plus side, their running apprehension work is outstanding. So is their search work. Sergeant Ron Shunk loves his Malinois K-9 Nero. I've watched Nero locate 9 millimeter shell casings in high grass and flatten most of the decoys on running apprehensions. Of the three I have observed, I would say Nero is the calmest and most relaxed. This trainer is familiar with Nero and says, "If they were all like Nero, I'd like them more than I do." It is my opinion that the other two are like they are because they are with

A well-built American Bulldog pup.

intimidating appearance they seem to make up for in performance. My only criticism is their size. All things being equal, I like a big dog if possible. There is an old saying:

"A good big man will beat a good little man every time."

I have personal experience with Rottweilers and considerable input from other sources. Doug Madigan, a civilian dog trainer, owned the first K-9-trained Rottie in Florida. This was as a result of a local police department being afraid to put the dog on the street. Someone had apparently overstressed the awesome power of the Rottweiler and had inadvertently talked themselves out of a K-9 Rottweiler for the time being. They later calmed the anxieties of the hierarchy and were able to put two Rotties on the street. The Rotties were feared by those who earned it and loved by the rest of us. My first K-9 was a Rottweiler named Zack. He was a house pet that was given to me. The extreme difficulty we experienced with him was due in part to our inexperience as trainers and to his being much too young. Rotties mature very slowly. The rest of the difficulty was due to his being a Rottweiler. They don't bounce back after tough corrections and sulk and pout and sometimes won't talk to you for days. On the plus side, they bite hard and have an excellent intimidation index (the ability to do crowd control simply by showing up). They are genuinely

inexperienced handlers. They all remind me of my dog Nick. I got him as a washout from another department because he was more or less uncontrollable. The former handler was not what you could call assertive. He was soft spoken and didn't convey the right message to the dog. The result was a dog that didn't have a lot of respect for the handler. I think the difference in these three Malinois is due more to the firm hand of Ron more than anything else. These dogs are simply more intent and require a firm handler, preferably a veteran. These dogs need to know who the boss is. Ron's dog knows. Put Nero in the hands of a wimpy handler and I think his excellent behavior would see a rapid decline.

These dogs average about 60 pounds. Whatever they lack in

scary looking. That alone is a valuable attribute when an officer finds himself suddenly surrounded by the friends of the guy that he just handcuffed. I've been there several times and the dog is why I'm writing this now instead of being a greasy spot at the corner of Fourth and Rardin.

Below is my personal ranking of dogs considered suitable for personal protection and police work. The top four I have owned personally. The fifth dog I have observed closely and can highly recommend. The first five on the list I recommend as police dogs. Others on the list can be used and some of them are being used as police dogs but I have no real experience with them.

*1. **AMERICAN BULLDOG** for reasons already noted. Affordable.

*2. **AMERICAN PIT BULL TERRIER** except for size, a near tie.

*3. **GERMAN SHEPHERD** a great dog, great coat, tough, trainable. Expensive.

*4. **ROTTWEILER** great dog, great coat, hard bite, intimidating, stubborn, wimpy handlers need not apply. Expensive.

*5. **BELGIAN MALINOIS** big dog in small package, good coat, when he's awake, he's wired! Not a dog for wimps. Very expensive.

6. **GIANT SCHNAUZER** reportedly being used in Germany with good results.

7. **BOUVIER DES FLANDRES** a fuzzy one but a good one. Used in Netherlands, Belgium.

8. **BULLMASTIFF** great puppy for reasons already noted. One of my personal favorites for a home guardian. Affordable.

9. **BELGIAN TERVUREN** hard dog, long hair, lightly built.

10. **BELGIAN SHEEPDOG** same comment.

11. **DOBERMAN PINSCHER** good ones are very rare hence their near extinction in police work in the U.S.

12. **KUVASZ** the only two I've seen were hard.

13. **NEAPOLITAN MASTIFF** every one I've seen was tough and protective.

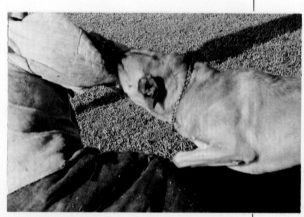

The author receiving a full mouth bite from K-9 Nero, a tough Belgian Malinois owned by Sergeant Ron Shunk.

14. **DOGUE DE BORDEAUX** never have seen one. See *Turner and Hooch* for a great look at the breed. They are reputed to be terrific dogs. Fairly affordable.

15. **PRESA CANARIO** resembles extra-large Pit Bull in many ways. Impressive looking dogs. Affordable.

Yes, there are probably more dogs that are supposed to be good guards but I can't verify this. I'm told by a trainer friend of mine

The Kuvasz, whose name derives from the Turkish word *kawasz*, which means "armed guard of the nobility," lives up to its name as a guardian breed. Photo by Isabelle Francais.

American breeds. They have more heart than anything else I'm aware of. When you combine that with the physical superiority of the Bulldog, there is just no comparison. Malinois are big dogs in small packages with lots of grit and determination, but the Bulldogs exceed this determination, are heavier and have about triple the physical strength. They deliver all that and are not wired all the time. They are relaxed, self-assured dogs that can be trusted with the family when not working. I say that for the following reason. A recent conversation with a respected trainer on the west coast was as much of a surprise as it was revealing. He is a Schutzhund trainer as well as Ringsport and K.N.P.V. His experience with both American Bulldogs and Malinois is extensive. He stated that he wouldn't own a Malinois for a

that the French Beauceron is a great one. If you'd like a close look at one rent the videotape *The Bear*. A pack of these dogs are used to hunt a bear in the movie and they look pretty good. They are advertised in *Dog World*. Another good guard dog is the Dutch Shepherd. I saw one doing K.N.P.V. on a tape recently. I couldn't begin to tell you where to find him other than Holland.

I admire a dog with determination. It is why I like the Malinois. When I watch them work, I get the impression that they will either get their man or die trying. I'd describe their commitment as nothing less than total. That commitment is exceeded only by the two

The Belgian Tervuren, a breed similar to the German Shepherd Dog, is agile and multi-talented, used worldwide as a police, military, and guide dog. Photo by Isabelle Francais.

house pet unless it was fully trained to out on command. According to him, the prey drive of these dogs is so intense that he fears they might go for anything making a quick move in front of them. He raises both of these breeds as well as others. Even though he gets much more money for the Malinois, his house dog is a protection-trained American Bulldog because it is laid back as opposed to the hair-trigger temperament of the Malinois.

My five-year-old boy is allowed to play unsupervised with my American Bulldog bitch because I know exactly what the outcome will be when Brent abuses her. Patch will flatten him and actually hold him down with her paws until I intervene or he quits. I don't intervene much anymore, and he doesn't complain much anymore because he knows he might be in as much trouble as she is. They play pretty rough sometimes, but she never gets carried away and has never so much as growled at him.

The biggest nagging doubt about this breed is what happens when your Bulldog meets another dog? Let me report that so far, there have been two incidents when outside and off lead, my dog has spotted a loose dog that snuck up on us unannounced and went after him. She recalled on verbal command, both times. Needless to say, I praised her highly for her good manners. Because of these successes, I'm going to try a new training technique I just learned, teaching the recall and out before the send

and bite. I'm told it works like a charm and with much less trauma to the dog.

When I began this book, I had witnessed only one American Bulldog doing protection work, my own. I had only caught one bulldog on a sleeve, Lance Jackson's Pit Bull, Rock. Rock is still the only Pit Bull I've trained.

The Belgian Sheepdog's inherent protective qualities and versatility make it an ideal watchdog and family guardian. Photo by Vince Serbin.

Physical differences aside, Rock had several things in common with American Bulldogs and Tom Bland's Mastiff. They all bit hard and required very little if any bite development work. I have since had three ABs visit me in the central Florida woods where I live. All three were tested in my back yard with a sleeve. All three passed with flying colors. With the exception of my bitch and a second bitch belonging to Sally Saxton, Chevy, all were quiet, placid dogs with very composed demeanors. The males were not barking at all the first time they saw a decoy making the sneaky aggressive approach. I was able to teach Rock to bark and he will now bark furiously at my approach. My bitch always did, and Chevy did. All the others,

a cable or chain, they stop slamming to the end of it in their attempts to trash the decoy. Every one of these dogs got back a few feet in an attempt to reel in the decoy within chain reach. This isn't sneaky or treacherous. This is smart. I drove all the way to northern Illinois to meet and test a possible stud dog named Bandit, an American Bulldog. He was raising hell when I pulled

The Presa Canario, or Canary Dog, has been described by many as an oversized version of the American Pit Bull Terrier. Photo by Isabelle Francais.

including Bullmastiffs, were silent. Wolf, the Mastiff, will give a small one with a little coercion from me. I get the impression that by and large the mastiff breeds are quiet dogs. Patience is another virtue of this group of dogs. Once they know they're on

into the yard. When I put the sleeve on and approached him, Bandit shut up real quick, got into a crouch and moved back a few feet. He wasn't looking for a place to run. He was coiled for a spring. His lower jaw was trembling and he was whining with anticipation. When he hit the sleeve it nearly knocked me over backwards. He shook me like a paint mixer.

As with all of the aforementioned Bulldogs, Bandit released the sleeve on his mistress's command. None of these dogs had to be pried off the sleeve. Bandit showed this controllability, yet the next day my right bicep and tricep as well as my rib cage were badly bruised from the sleeve slamming back and forth on my arm. However, I was able to pet Bandit as soon as it was over. This is what is known as a dual personality. It is exactly what you are looking for in a protection dog of any breed because you will be able to control him at all times. This is the type of personality that will allow you to take your protection dog into a crowded public place off lead and not worry about him attacking someone simply because they walked within reach. The dog only reacts to aggressive behavior.

The trip to Rode Hawg Kennels to see Bandit was worth every penny. It resulted in a litter of 13 healthy pups that fear nothing. This is interesting because Bandit's original owner got rid of him because he labeled him as "man shy."

One other thing that these dogs have in common—there was no need to teach them to bite. The rag was not used at all on any of these dogs. They were not encouraged to bite. They were simply given the

Once a popular guarding breed, the Doberman Pinscher has lost popularity as a police dog because it is so difficult to find one with the correct temperament for training. Photo by Isabelle Francais.

opportunity to bite and they all did. These dogs were developed for their natural biting talents and ability as canine gladiators.

One other reason you might consider training your dog is that it will in all likelihood make him a very happy dog. It has been my experience that nothing rounds out a dog quite like protection training. Taking your dog with you at every opportunity helps broaden his map of the world but nowhere near the extent of protection training. When the dog is agitated, it causes a certain amount of stress that is released when he is allowed to bite the bad guy. Releasing stress helps calm his nerves just as it does in humans. Biting is his most important method of stress relief. After K-9 training my dog was always drained. It wasn't just the physical stress of tracking, agility, building searches, running attack, etc., but the mental stress that went along with it. Anticipation caused his stress. Trashing baddies was his release from this stress. After a four- or five-hour training session he was always spent and would sleep like a dead dog. The next day he was charged and ready for action. He would demand that I play with him, take him for a ride, a walk or *something*. He was filled with nervous energy to the point of overflowing. What he liked best, of course, was K-9 training. He knew that he would get to hunt a creep and vanquish him by biting him and shaking him silly. The only

experience in life that could exceed this adrenaline rush was getting a late-night phone call on our nights off. This always meant a manhunt. The only people that ever called at 2:00 in the morning were police dispatchers and my dog Nick knew this. Having had numerous real bites to his credit, Nick knew the difference. Nothing in the known universe could equal the pleasure that Nick would derive from a real bite on a real bad guy.

Nick knew that a late-night phone call would result in a real bite. We were always on call and the competition knew when our days off would occur. They seemed to arrange their crimes accordingly. Most of the armed robberies, shootings, burglaries, rapes and murders occurred on our nights off. We took this as a compliment. Even on my nights

Ch. Sultan of Vanguard Kennels, a 165-pound blue male Neapolitan Mastiff.

off, I wouldn't turn in before 4:00 a.m. I couldn't sleep if I did. It would almost guarantee that something would go bump in the night.

Dogs are social animals and team hunters. The most similar scenario that most people will be able to create for their dogs as far as going on a hunt (the ultimate doggy adrenaline rush) is to invite them to load up in the family sedan and ride shotgun on a trip to the grocery store, post office or to pick up the kids after baseball practice. You may have already noticed how he thinks this is the best idea you've had all day. The only dog owners who might have seen more excitement in a dog are real hunters loading their hunting dogs into the truck to go on a *real* hunting trip, or a Schutzhund person asking their dog if they want to go train, or a police officer asking his K-9 the same question. On the way to the destination, you'll see the static electricity building up to overflowing. It grounds out by barking, whining, and howling. Sometimes Nick would nip my knees prior to the gunfire attack portion of a police dog competition even though he knew I'd clobber him for it. He couldn't help it. His effervescent static electricity was simply arcing onto the nearest object he could touch with his vibrating front teeth. He was stressed by the anticipation of getting to bite someone who richly deserved it. The decoy always said Nick did his hardest biting during gunfire

The Dogue de Bordeaux, or French Mastiff, is an ancient breed known throughout the ages as a hunter, guardian, baiter, and fighter. This dog's intelligence and large size were recently displayed in the U.S.A. on the big screen. Photo by Isabelle Francais.

attack. This is where the most stress was for this dog and where he needed the most stress relief, which resulted in Nick's most strenuous efforts to rid the planet of the scourge known as decoys.

With all of the foregoing information about Nick, one might ascertain that Nick was a borderline uncontrollable dog most of the time. Just the opposite. He was completely controllable at all times (nearly). Because of his extensive training and street experience, he developed an arrogant confidence that almost was a swagger. Experienced, older police dogs develop this level of confidence to the point where when they are facing a potential bad guy they no longer bark at him. They simply give him a look. It is quite unnerving. With any good guard breed this confidence level will develop with age and experience. With American Bulldogs it is a birthright.

Bottom line? A working dog is a happy dog. Whether he's trashing bad guys or just going along for the ride, he's getting rid of built-up stress. The family pet who doesn't do bitework releases his stress by yapping at passing trucks or treeing the neighbor's cat. Either way, it results in a happy dog. Stress-free dogs are healthier dogs. They live longer—same with humans. Working out relieves stress in humans and is being recommended with an ever-increasing frequency by doctors nowadays.

My current protector will actually come and get me and tell me whether she wants to walk, run or train. If she wants to come along for the ride, she lets me know by loading into the truck when I open the door. She wakes me precisely at 8:00 each morning (give or take five minutes) by shaking her head and making her ears flap loudly.

One quiet bark gets her out the door to relieve herself. A growl at the screen door or a window gets her back in the house. She goes for walks, runs, rides and gets to rough up a decoy at least once a week. She is free of parasites, allergies, breathing and bone problems. She's alert, healthy, stress-free and very happy.

In case there is any lingering doubt in the reader's mind, perhaps the following will convince you. I've been training an American Bulldog for the past month. When he was first introduced to me, he lunged for me. His owner told me that this was the dog's normal behavior—if he was on lead, he felt he should bite anyone within six feet of his owner. Off lead he was much more relaxed. He was aloof to anyone but family, and wouldn't attack you if you kept your distance. Once the lead was snapped to his collar he once again became overly protective. I explained to his owner that the dog was sensing his tension by smell and by body language. Expecting the dog to bristle up, Tom would choke up on the leash at the approach of an innocent stranger. American Bulldogs, remember, are gladiators. Reading body language is very important when combat is your vocation. It will telegraph the hostile intentions of an adversary. Prey drive also was coming into play with this man/dog team. Since dogs hunt as a pack, they pick up on any change in their fellow pack member's behavior. When Tom's tension made him choke up on the leash, Preacher read this as "Tom is tensed for trouble. Tom is ready for action." Well, Preacher wasn't about to miss a chance to protect his best friend. He went into action thinking that Tom was about to. When the leash was off the dog, he couldn't feel Tom choking up on the leash at the approach of a stranger, therefore, he was more relaxed and more tolerant of the stranger. Not to the point that he would allow the stranger to approach him and pet him, but the stranger was at least safe from attack if he obeyed the simple rule of staying six feet away from him or Tom.

Thirty days later we were into running attack (off lead), tracking, hurdles, article search, obedience, etc.

The dog outed verbally the very first time and every time since. On his second day of bitework we introduced him to a full bite suit. There was absolutely no hesitation about biting any part of the body. It did take a full ten days before Preacher would allow me to *touch* him, let alone pet him.

We reached the point where I could come in on him, get thoroughly destroyed, drop the sleeve, come back in a passive manner, squat down and he'd knock me over, licking my face.

We procured three new decoys who were curious about the breed and the training. We went to a city park where I gave detailed instructions to our three volunteers. The dogs had been hitting well enough, but weren't getting the deep bites I required. I

Giants Apache Renegade. This pup may turn out to be the largest purebred registered APBT in existence. Shown here at 8 months and 105 pounds!

decided we needed more room for longer runs and faster runners. The park and the new decoy were the answer. The hits and bites were devastating. The younger men were definitely faster, which really got our dogs' drives percolating. Then I saw something that really frightened me—one of our new decoys got down in a crouch and was baby-talking Preacher with outstretched arms. Before I could yell a warning, Preacher was on him! Licking his face, knocking him down and sitting in his lap. Thirty days of bitework had drained whatever stress there was in Preacher and taught him confidence. He still does an occasional lunge for what I call "squirrelly" people.

These are the overly humane-

American Bulldog—the author's top choice for K-9 protection.

type people who believe they can visit Kenya and get out of their car and pet the lions because their hearts are filled with nothing but good intentions. These people will try to pet a formidable-looking dog even though they're scared out of their wits. These people suffer from what I call "FDR syndrome." FDR (President Franklin Delano Roosevelt) is the man who said, "The only thing we have to fear is fear itself." These people suffering from FDR syndrome want to stoically force themselves to face their fears. What they don't realize is that they reek of fear. Their body language is furtive, fearful and can, in some instances, even appear sneaky. This is exactly what I do when testing a green dog to see if he will bite me.

When you see this type of character approaching with a trembling hand extended toward the dog simply hold the dog tightly. You can issue a warning that the dog may bite or you can let the dog issue the warning. Either way they will eventually remember that they had something on the stove at home or find some other reason to leave. When my dog goes off on these people I don't correct her and don't require Tom to correct Preacher for a similar reaction. These people are acting exactly like a sneaky thief. The dog is only doing his job. Fortunately, people suffering from FDR syndrome are indeed rare. Most fearful people will simply stay away from your dog.

Eventually, Preacher will be able to walk at a perfect heel on Tom's left side off lead through a crowded supermarket at 5:30 p.m. without Tom worrying about the dog's behavior. More of the forced socialization that I've prescribed with corrections for lunges or even growls at peaceful strangers will eventually result in this ability. Had Preacher been in less capable hands and not received protection training, he might very well have become a hideous liability to his owner.

Protection training doesn't make dogs mean, just the opposite. It teaches them confidence, which results in dogs that are dependable, calm and stable—a quiet companion capable of saving your life or the lives of the entire family.

Socialization

Socialization is an essential ingredient for any type of training, but most especially when protection-training your dog.

Socialization of our training candidate is of paramount importance. As the new handler takes his new charge with him in all his daily activities, the dog learns to interact with his environment. Above all the dog must be stable, calm and tolerant of people he may meet daily. The dog was chosen for his disposition. He must be friendly but also fearless. This is what we call a dual-personality dog. His aggression should surface only when needed. During this period the dog learns that most people are nice. Some aren't, but that will be learned later. At this time we want him to experience as many different surfaces as possible and be relaxed on all of them. Some of these surfaces will include asphalt, concrete, tile, grass, wood, gravel, steel grate, carpet, sand, astro-turf, rock, etc.

Our K-9 bodyguard should also experience all the modes of transportation that his new role might require. He should be an accomplished swimmer because he may have to swim a canal or creek during a manhunt or chase a man into the surf to apprehend him. He must meet lots of people (children included). He should meet other dogs and be discouraged from showing any aggression towards them or any other animals. This applies to the various bulldog breeds especially. (Remember, catching livestock is their vocation.) Attempts to catch livestock should be met with heavy corrections. We don't want our dogs chasing cats when they're supposed to be chasing burglars, so make sure you don't forget to introduce him to our feline friends. Working dogs will have strong prey drives and cats are in their food chain.

During socialization the dog shouldn't be left alone with strangers or (especially) small children. Don't panic. The dog will probably behave just fine, but don't trust humans. Small

Socialization begins during puppyhood.

children have a propensity toward cruelty when left unsupervised with pets. Remember, most police/ protection dog candidates were chosen because of their inborn trait to defend themselves against the aggressive human. Some dogs are even imported with Schutzhund titles (which means they're professional biters). Responsibility for the dog's behavior rests squarely on the shoulders of the dog's master. A responsible adult doesn't leave a loaded gun lying around the house. The same common sense will apply where the dog is concerned. If children are in the household, they should be read the riot act where the dog is concerned and thoroughly educated as to how he is treated. This is especially important when a grown dog is being introduced to the family. Once he has accepted them as his family, there will be no problem. Supervision is recommended for the first two weeks so that any behavior problems (human or canine) can be nipped in the bud. Example: don't allow your eight-month-old to crawl over to the dish while the new dog is eating. Seems like common sense would prevent a tragedy in a case like that, but I'm aware of it happening in real life. The baby's face was ripped and they kept the dog. Neither the baby nor the dog was to blame in that situation. It was about the third day with the new owners. I have photos of my baby boy looking down my K-9's throat like a lion tamer. That kind of trust and familiarity doesn't come overnight, but it *does* come.

There will always be days when things aren't going as well as you'd like. If you show up at the training field in an ugly mood, your dog will notice it as quickly as a human would. When you're in such a mood, it might be better to give the dog the day off. When you're under stress, your temper gets short and your patience wears thin. Believe it or not, stress is contagious. If you're stressed out on training day, stay home. In fact stay home and play with your dog. Try this: lay face down on your carpet and cup both hands over your face. He'll wonder what the hell you are doing and will attempt to get between your face and the carpet. Thinking you're trying to

Above: Expose your dog to as many different people as possible, however...**Below:** ...be sure to supervise very young children as they have a propensity toward cruelty and teasing when left alone with a pet.

Above: This picture was made for those who believe that protection training makes your dog mean. The five-year-old is the author's son Brent. He knows Rock, but seldom sees him. The photo was taken right after Rock shook the author's fillings loose on the sleeve. Yes, Brent could sit on Patch, too, but any kid can sit on their own dog, right?

hide something from him, he will go nuts trying to pry your face off the carpet. If you can keep from laughing during this frenzy, you've either got a lot of self control or no sense of humor. When you're down on the floor like this, you're down on his level and he's really glad you came down. If you like having him on your lap but can't tolerate the hair on the

Left: Pete Curley's Presa Canario, a 135-lb bitch.

furniture, get on the floor. No dog can resist a human on the floor and they will come over and cheer you up real quick. They will nuzzle and lick all the stress off your face. I have two stress relievers in my life. They are my five-year-old son, Brent, and my one-year-old daughter, Patch (an American Bulldog).

Right: Interaction with children is very important when socializing a guard dog. **Below:** RIVER PIRATES! The two stress relievers in author Mike Harlow's life: his son Brent and his American Bulldog Patch.

Obedience

Obedience training is the prerequisite for all other types of training and is the foundation of control. Without control over your protection-trained dog, you could find yourself with major legal problems. Photo of "Spanky" taken by his owner, Sue Miller.

INTRODUCTION

I have taught obedience (OB) to all of my dogs and to other dogs, and I often hear comments on how smart the dogs are. I agree that dogs are pretty smart but the real credit is due to the hard work and commitment of the owner. It just takes a little perseverance to eventually program the dog's brain into believing that deviating from the master's wishes is to experience some form of unpleasantness. Ideally, the dog eventually makes the connection that it's easier as well as quicker to do it your way. He makes this connection more quickly if you are consistent and firm with corrections. Firm corrections require very few repetitions, and make deeper impressions in the dog's memory bank. Corrections are done with the aid of a choke chain and a six-foot leather leash. Properly done corrections leave the dog thinking he was responsible for the pain that resulted when he made a left turn as you made a right turn. You were ready for the jolt and he was not because he wasn't paying attention. On-lead OB training will have the dog paying close attention in a relatively short amount of time, *if* you do your part.

CORRECTION

Some of the people I've helped blanched at the thought of administering a tough correction and quit the class rather than put the dog through the trauma of the correction phase. I say phase because it's a passing thing. Eventually the dog makes the correction and requires no more corrections. I think one woman who quit the class was under the impression that dog obedience meant a lifetime of rough treatment for her dog. Perhaps I failed to make it sufficiently clear that the correction phase was just that: a phase. Her dog is very small, yet drags her everywhere. She is comfortable with that because she knows she won't have to hurt her dog with any corrections.

With a 12-pound dog I guess that's a tolerable state of affairs. For a dog big enough to be a protection dog, it's not. This is why the OB phase is done first. If you don't have the intestinal fortitude to do the required corrections here, you have no business owning a large

Two well-behaved protection dogs sit calmly for the camera. The dog on the right is an American Bulldog-Dogue de Bordeaux cross owned by John Blackwell.

formidable dog, and don't even think about protection work!

LIABILITY

Obedience is the foundation of control and if you don't have complete control of your big, strong, protection-trained dog, you stand an excellent chance of losing most of your net worth to one of the civil liability sharks that pervade our society and you just might deserve to.

To tackle bitework without the control learned in obedience would be viewed by a plaintiff's council as a perfect example of culpable negligence on your part. Let's assume for a minute that your mutt did something really unspeakable to a burglar that he caught red-handed inside your house. That he not only stopped him but savaged him for ten minutes while you tried unsuccessfully to pry him off. In court, numerous self-professed dog trainers testify that protection training is actually a series of training phases starting with "socialization," "obedience," then "bitework," in that order. Now armed with expert testimony, plaintiff's (victim's) council asks if you subjected your dog to all the prerequisite phases. If you answer yes, you are now guilty of perjury in addition to the aggravated battery charge and they will prove it with the greatest of ease. You could even be charged with a civil rights violation of denying the burglar due process in that your maniac dog punished him without benefit of a trial (this really happened). If you say your dog is controllable, you will be given a chance to prove it. However, you won't be given the opportunity to rehearse the demonstration of Fido's controllability. In the meantime, he'll languish in a filthy cage at the pound being fed the cheapest chow the government can find. He will probably be next to a street cur that has parvo or rabies or distemper. If your dog fails to show acceptable control he will probably be destroyed and you will then be bled dry by the court and your defense attorney. If your dog does the ultimate unspeakable act, you are almost guaranteed a jail sentence.

So go ahead and skip the obedience section if you think it's wise, but I strongly urge you to take the time required to make your dog into a trustworthy, dependable, controllable tool instead of a real nuisance.

Don't come down with civil liability paranoia due to this warning. Keeping a protection-trained dog can be a worry-free proposition with the application of just a little common sense. It is practically the same drill that owners of American Pit Bull Terriers observe. You *know* what you have. Simply be responsible.

1. Don't let the dog roam.

2. When the dog is in his yard he should be fenced for the safety of people having a legitimate reason for being in your yard: mail carrier, fireman, policeman, neighbor.

Irresponsible owners are to blame for the current bad reputation of the Pit Bull. These dogs are among the most people-friendly breeds in existence. Their behavior around other dogs is predictable; they have a propensity toward fighting. This is common knowledge, yet some idiots fail to take the necessary precautions for the safe keeping of this fine breed. The result is the bad reputation and legislation aimed at the extinction of the breed. Irresponsible ownership can result in a similar dilemma for police and protection-trained dogs. Don't allow it to happen.

NON-COMMUNICATIVE TECHNIQUE

Much of what you read in the obedience section might begin to sound pretty familiar to some of the salty old dog people out there, especially if they've read Bill Koehler's book on guard dog training. I quote him shamelessly in more than one place in this book and haven't the slightest fear of anyone yelling plagiarism because I give him full credit for most of my knowledge on obedience training and I recommend his book. Though written about 30 years ago, it is still useful and accurate. I see no reason to deviate from his methods of teaching OB. His methods work and as the U.S. Army says, "If it ain't broke, don't fix it."

One point he only touches on lightly, which I would like to emphasize, is starting the dog walking on a leash. Bill labeled it non-communicative walking. It means you don't talk to the dog during the exercise at all. No verbal communication whatsoever! The idea is that you are not scolding him or making him aware that you're displeased in any way. If he hears no voice communication from you at all, he won't think his mishap was caused by you or that you are angry with him. This way he won't develop an aversion to the leash or to the walks. What will happen is he will think it was his fault (and it was). He will eventually make the connection that the safest place for him to be when walking is at your side. He will make the connection that the *only* way for him to avoid the jolting U-turn is to keep an eye on you. He can't do that while

Giants' Gladiator Thor, a red nose APBT weighing 75 pounds at ten months with his owners, who also have an infant son. This dog was obedience- and protection-trained by Bob Warren K-9 Academy in Massachusetts. Bred by Land of Giants APBT kennel.

walking in front of you. I'll caution the reader that if you ignore his method you may spend lots of time on OB and teach your dog to hate the sessions as well. If you can ignore the temptation to yak at the dog while you're yanking him around on a leash, you will save yourself a *lot* of time. These learning sessions will perhaps be a little startling, but not frightening. If you are yelling "heel" every time you yank the leash, you will invariably wind up saying it through clenched teeth, which

Sugar and Mindy (littermates) won 1st and 2nd place at obedience school out of 15 other dogs of various breeds.

will make the dog think you are angry at him. When he becomes frightened, it's time to stop. While frightened he will be unable to do anything right and you will just get more disgusted. Losing your temper will only set you further back. The non-communicative walking and surprise U-turn method of getting the dog's attention is by far the best and quickest method. My problem is not with Mr. Koehler's method but with his conservative estimate of how long it takes the dog to become attentive and start watching you. He says four days. The last one I did took about eight minutes! I have a problem with another time estimate and I hope it's a misprint. He states that from starting leash training to graduating to the off-lead phase should take no less than 13 weeks. I've seen mature dogs start from scratch, do everything in this book and graduate training in 12 weeks. If 13 weeks is an accurate figure for the on-lead OB phase, I guess we could count on the dog graduating the complete police K-9 school in about a year! I hope that 13-week figure was a misprint because Mr. Koehler's OB methods work *much* more quickly than that, especially if you're starting with a mature dog. It took me exactly eight weeks to train my current pup, who was six months old when I started her. I realize I can no longer be considered an amateur handler, but I am not a professional trainer either.

That brings me to another subject. Beware of bogus trainers. There's a lot of them out there. There doesn't seem to be any law out there mandating graduation from an approved course of dog training, so a lot of clowns simply ordain themselves dog trainers. If you do seek out the services of a professional, ask to see some credentials. If he has any, he'll be happy to show them off. When you go to his office, home or kennel, look for trophies, plaques, diplomas, press clippings or whatever. If I was planning to become a professional trainer, I would certainly have something to show off besides a business card and a sleeve. Check them out before writing a check. Ask for references. The woman who quit my class spent $300 on obedience lessons on her dog before she met me. I saw no evidence of training on her dog.

EQUIPMENT RECOMMENDATIONS

I recommend *only* leather leashes and collars. The reason is simple. They last. The only other material worthy of mention is nylon. It is the strongest material in the world for making collars and leashes, but it will fray and unravel. All of them are sewn together and with the normal rough treatment they will see (especially police K-9), the stitching will be the first thing to go, leaving you with a mess. Buy a top-quality leather leash (six feet) with a solid brass snap. I have a short leather traffic lead that I bought 20 years ago and I'm still using it every day. I paid top dollar for it but I've never had to replace it. Perhaps once a year (if I remember) I rub a *little* neat's-foot oil into it. It may never die. Yes, I own nylon long lines and a few super shorties with quick release bull snaps (panic snaps), but every six-foot training leash and every collar I've made is of top-quality, top-grain cowhide. Brass hardware will outlast nickel-plated iron or steel. It won't rust and doesn't require oiling.

Lots of people make choke chains. The only ones I can recommend are made in Germany. Each link is welded and they are heavily chrome plated. They work smoothly and will outlast any dog. All of the better K-9 equipment catalogues carry them. You will never find them in a grocery

Soft padded agitator collar made out of the finest leather by the author.

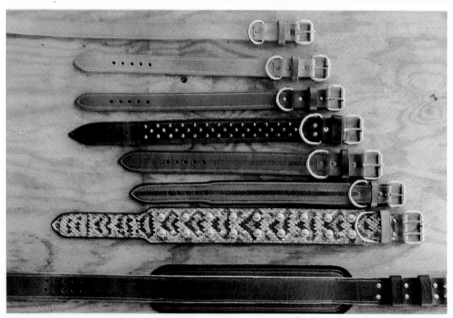

For serious dogs, use serious leather collars.

store or pet shop. These K-9 equipment catalogues are also excellent sources of all kinds of quality equipment for all kinds of dogs. If you are starting a K-9 unit or Schutzhund club you will need equipment. All of it can be found in these catalogues. Sleeves, bite suits, muzzles, leashes, harnesses, collars, toys and even bulletproof vests for your favorite dog.

The two leather collars I made eight years ago for K-9 Nick are being worn proudly today by Patch, my American Bulldog. Both collars look like they've got at least another 12 years left in them.

HEELING

Find a large open field in which to train. School campuses are ideal as well as parks. It is nice if you can get several people to train with you so that your dog can start with plenty of distractions. He must learn to interact with other dogs eventually and now is as good a time to start as any. The first thing we will teach him is proper heeling. The only equipment necessary will be the six-foot leather leash and the choke chain. It should be the smallest size that you can still fit over his head. The rings must be on the dog's right side. The dog will always be walked on your left. His right shoulder will be even with the handler's left leg. He should be no more than a few inches away from the handler's leg. The different ways in which he will avoid the proper heel are as follows:

1. LAGGING light jerk on lead while patting your left leg. Verbal encouragement may also help.

2. SURGING the surprise U-turn.

3. CROWDING apply knee to dog's shoulder—failing this, attach a pinbrush to the knee with duct tape and repeat.

4. SHYING AWAY verbal encouragement, pat the leg—failing this, sharp jerk on lead, verbal *no*, verbal "heel."

5. SITTING verbal encouragement, patting the leg.

6. LYING DOWN verbal encouragement, patting the leg.

9. BITING HANDLER a hanging offense.

Reward a good performance with verbal praise. Nothing more is necessary nor recommended. Don't create a dog that will only behave for treats. Petting the dog or hugging the dog is even stronger praise and should be used only when he has accomplished something in an exemplary manner, usually at the end of an exercise. Praise is your dog's

A strong leather leash is the most basic form of equipment you will need when training your dog.

7. BOLTING neckbreaker of a snatch in the other direction resulting in a back flip if possible. (Hard corrections don't need many repeats.)

8. CLIMBING HANDLER apply your knee very hard to his chest and reinforce it with a stern verbal *"no."*

reward for pleasing you. We can accomplish nearly anything with it. The best type of verbal praise is done in as high a voice as you can muster and it should mimic exactly how we talk to babies. The dogs respond to this tone in a big way, since they can't understand our speech.

You might feel a little silly at first talking to a dog in such a stupid fashion, but after you see the improved response it elicits from the dog, you won't think it's stupid at all.

Not only will verbal praise be relied on in the OB phase but we will rely on it throughout every phase of this training.

U-TURN

During the on-lead OB phase, we will let the dog teach himself by making his own mistakes and suffering the inevitable discomfort that will *consistently* follow his mistakes.

Sure-Grip's Rattler weighing 91 pounds at eight months. This dog performed in the role of "Chance" in the movie *Incredible Journey* (1992).

Translation: When he is out in front of you, a quick U-turn is done while maintaining the same momentum and holding the leash firmly against your belt buckle in both hands. It could very well result (hopefully) in your dog doing a back flip with a poor landing. This maneuver should be done without so much as a peep out of you and you should keep going in your intended direction until you have covered, say, 50 feet. If the last 30 feet were done with the dog flopped on his side, it's not your fault and don't you dare feel guilty and stop. He will eventually find this technique less tolerable than you do and will either get up and walk or regain his feet when you've covered your intended 50 feet.

THE LEFT TURN

To accomplish a left turn one must pivot on the left toe and swing the right knee around to take the next step. If your dog was leading, he caught the knee in the chops or side. Good. If it was done with gusto, better. He'll learn it more quickly. A few repetitions and he'll be paying closer attention. When he does it well, give V.P. The lead is held in the right hand at about the three-foot level and about six inches to the front. Looping the leash over the thumb allows you to administer the proper correction without hurting your hand and to choke up on the normal amount of slack in the leash when Fido is heeling correctly.

A word of caution: About 15 minutes of this is all you want to do on the dog's first session. If he is a puppy, don't start him at all until he has reached six months of age. Dogs are babies before six months and need all the hugs and kisses that a human baby needs. At six

months you can start light OB doing basic turns and heeling. When he reaches a year you can commence more serious OB work. Let him grow up first.

If he is leading you when you're trying to do the left turn make it a memorable left turn by pivoting on your left foot and swinging your right knee into his midsection with gusto! Properly done, it should get a good grunt out of him. Make sure you are looking straight ahead when you do this and continue on in your intended direction as though nothing happened. Again, you want to convey the message to him that you aren't displeased in the least. He will think it was his fault (and it was). He will be paying close attention after a couple of those and that's exactly what we are trying to accomplish. You can't teach him anything until you have his attention. He will have to watch you to determine what your next directional change will be and he can't do it while he's out in front of you. He will have to be at your side to avoid being trampled on the left turn and he will have to be at your side to avoid a jolting back flip when you do your non-communicative quick U-turn. These two techniques will quickly produce a dog that walks downfield looking into your eyes for the next telltale sign that you are about to change direction. After

surprisingly few back flips and tramplings, he really is concerned about your next change of direction. This entire routine is done with a slack leash. Your signal to commence the U-turn is when Fido takes up the slack by forging ahead, pulling you along behind. If he's leading only slightly, this is your cue to the pivoting left turn. Remember, no communication during this session. You don't want him thinking you are mad at him or he'll develop an aversion to training and/or the leash.

THE RIGHT TURN

This is very easy. Again, pivot on your left toe and take a big step to the right with your right foot. At the same time you give a sharp jerk on the lead in the direction of travel. If the dog wasn't paying attention a couple of repeated turns should get the desired results. If all of the foregoing didn't get his attention, it's time to resort to a little power steering. The prong or pinch collar is a bit more of an attention getter. Corrections done with it are three times more effective and believe me, you will meet dogs that require it as a routine measure. Some trainers use it exclusively when starting dogs. We will see it used extensively during bitework for control. Don't let the sight of it scare you. Dogs have unbelievably tough necks— your own experience will reinforce what I tell you. The exaggerated steps in the turns

The spiked collar is effective protection against bad guys who may try to grab and injure your police/guard dog.

Trained dogs are happy dogs. Obedience training builds self-esteem and confidence.

taken with your right foot have a definite purpose. It allows your dog to read some very obvious body language. It warns him of your intentions and allows him to prepare for the turn instead of having you step on him. Use this exaggerated step. It's like a turn signal.

THE SIT

The dog should automatically come to a sit every time you stop. To accomplish this feat of derring-do, you gently pull straight up on the leash while gently pressing on his rear. Failing this, use more force. Of course all of this is preceded by the word "sit." Verbal praise is in order when his butt hits the deck, whether it was his idea or yours.

THE STAY

With the dog on lead and walking on your left, sweep your right hand around in a c-shaped arc into but not touching his nose. This should be done in a very exaggerated movement with the palm of your hand facing him (fingers pointing upwards). At the same time, say the word "stay" in a loud commanding voice. This is

Bulldog sitting obediently at attention. Banuelos' Predator SchHII wearing the author's trophy collar.

to confuse him momentarily. The combination of your hand in his face and the extra-loud command makes him hesitate for a couple seconds and before he can sort it out and follow, you tell him in no uncertain terms "Good Boy!" and give him a hug. He'll learn this one quickly and you will eventually (over a few weeks) be able to widen the gap between you and your dog until you are completely out of your dog's sight for several minutes.

THE DOWN

This is probably the toughest thing in the OB phase. In the dog world it is an act of submission. The tougher the dog, the tougher it is to teach. With the dog at a sit, you bend down, point to the ground in an exaggerated motion and firmly

give the command "down." If he does it (which I doubt) give him praise. When he refuses, repeat the command while jerking down on the leash. When this fails, stomp on the leash about one foot from his neck while booming the command "down" He can't help but go down, but he just might get up after you get off the leash. If his reluctance is accentuated with a growl, don't wait to see what he's going to do next. Go directly to your hardware store and buy a heavy eyebolt. Now go back to the training field and find a large tree with a large visible root sticking a little above the ground. Screw the eyebolt into the root (all the way). Now thread your leash through the eyebolt and hook it to the tough guy's collar. Now scream the command *"DOWN!!!"* like you mean it and yank up hard on that leash! His chin will hit the deck with authority. This technique should almost never be necessary with a dog you raised from a puppy. But if you are a cop and are starting a tough dog imported from the Fatherland, he may be cranky from his trip or he may just be testing you. Either way he's got to hit the deck before you go much further. What we are trying to avoid here is you getting bitten. It is a distinct possibility. This method will allow you to slam him down (which is necessary) without having him give you the new look. It is extremely doubtful that you will get another challenge out of that dog because you've just shown him his place in the pack. This method is completely safe for even the greenest of handlers.

THE COME

Possibly the most important command in this phase is "come." If your dog won't come to you when you call him, he will probably disobey most other commands when off lead. Therefore it is imperative that he learn it well and learn it early. When you call him make it loud enough for him to hear, but don't scare him with it. You don't want him to think he's in trouble. Remember, he doesn't understand 99 percent of the language, just tones. Make sure he hears a tone that conveys that you're happy, not angry, no matter how angry you really are. Your tone should be telling him he's going to receive praise (and he is). A good method of getting him running your way is to run from him after making sure he's looking at you. If he's not looking in your direction, he

Nobody but nobody is going to harm **this** pretty lady. Lauren Goldman of L.A. with her dog, Giants Black Sabbath at 19 months and 104 pounds, from Giants kennel in Massachusetts.

won't see you trying to outrun him. When he sees you running, he won't be able to resist the challenge. When he gets close, turn and face him, bent over and with arms outstretched, and make sure he gets a big hug. *Never* call him to a beating. He will only come once, if he has any intelligence. If your reward for a maximum effort in the 100-yard dash was a punch in the mouth, you'd quickly lose your enthusiasm for the 100-yard dash. *Beating your dog will be unnecessary and uncalled for throughout this training.* It will in fact set you back and not accomplish a damn thing. Don't do it. All the corrections you'll need are listed as they become necessary.

THE NO

This is a very important command. It is used to make the dog stop whatever he is doing. It is spoken very decisively and with some volume. If the dog is attempting

Sure Grip kennel's Freddie Krueger. This well-trained dog was featured in the Disney movie *Bingo.*

to start a fight with another dog, *"NO!"* and a neck breaker yank on the leash should suffice. If he wants to eat a dead rat, *"NO!"* Taste a scorpion, *"NO!"* Chase a cat, *"NO!"*, etc.

HEEL FROM A DISTANCE OR COMING TO A HEEL

The dog can be in a "sit," a "down," a "stand," or on a break and when told to heel, should come to the handler and wind up sitting at a perfect heel on the handler's side (left side). There are two methods of teaching the "heel." The first is the military method. With the dog in a "sit-stay," the handler steps out to the full length of the six-foot lead and faces his dog. With the lead held in your left hand, give your dog the command to heel. At the same time, reach out with your right hand and pull the dog towards your right side, around behind you passing the leash from right hand to left hand, and stopping the dog in the proper position at your left side. He should sit without command but be prepared to give it if necessary. The dog will handle this clumsily at first. Be patient. Remember, this is new to him. He's not refusing. He just doesn't know what you want. Once he knows, he will comply. Let him know he's a good boy.

The American Kennel Club method is easier to teach and smarter to use in my opinion. The handler is facing his dog six feet away (on lead). Give heel command. Left foot takes

Giants Hagar. Male at 12 months, 95 pounds. Obedience- and protection-trained. Lives with family with children as pet and guardian in France. Bred by Land of Giants.

BIG back step. Left hand reaches out and grabs leash midway. Pull leash in a horizontal arc to the left. The dog will follow. Now place left foot back even with the right foot pulling the dog with you in a perfect heel. Give the sit command if necessary and lots of praise. In essence the dog has done a tight U-turn slightly behind you and come to a "heel," and you never had to pass the leash behind you. Passing the leash behind you is a pain and the military method seems to encourage the dog to circle the handler when given the command to straighten up his "heel." The AKC method eliminates the need to play "pass the leash" and dogs taught in this method don't circle the handler when told to straighten up or when nervous. A dog circling the handler's legs during a riot or crowd situation can be disastrous, hence only the AKC method can be recommended. Having attended no less than six riots and numerous crowd situations with a leg-circling dog, I feel my opinion is authoritative.

OFF-LEAD OBEDIENCE

Nearly all the commands for "on-lead" OB are done in an identical manner for the off-lead phase except the leash is disconnected. If the dog shows reluctance simply hook him up and give him a refresher with a couple of harsh corrections. One or two refreshers should be all that's necessary. Don't forget to praise the good performance.

The exaggerated left-foot backstep of the AKC come-to-a-heel may gradually be dropped, as the dog will eventually get the message when he sees the

"Whiskey" guarding his home. Thieves would be wise to pass up this balcony and keep on going.

left hand making its horizontal arc to the left or when he hears the verbal command to heel.

All commands should first be done verbally *and* by hand. After much repetition the dog will respond to hand signals only. When he backslides, refresh his memory with the combination of both hand signals and verbal commands. Don't forget to reward the good performance.

PATIENCE IN OBEDIENCE TRAINING

If all of these obedience exercises seem a bit oversimplified, perhaps they are. Or perhaps other people have taken something simple and made it difficult by lengthening it.

My opinion is that OB is simple and easy. If it's frustrating you, take a break. Think about what you're doing. Ask yourself: Am I losing my temper with this stupid dog? If the answer is "yes," don't feel alone. We do lose our tempers. I know because I have the patience of Job, for about three seconds. Yes, I have lost my temper while training and it has never failed to set me back. Remember that the dog doesn't know what you want. Your job is to show him without intimidating him. It is impossible to give your dog too much praise. Don't forget it! He hasn't the mental capacity to become vain. Lay on the praise like he was your firstborn son taking his first step.

Plenty of repetition is required but care must be taken to avoid doing too much of the same thing at once. Dogs get bored too. Provide some breaks in the monotony and always end a training session on a good note, even if you must regress to a really simple task that you know the dog can do blindfolded. *Do it.* In this way the dog can quit a winner and know he pleased you. If a training session ends with a correction and a scolding, guess what the dog will remember at the beginning of the next session? We don't want to reward a poor performance, so go to a simpler task that you know will produce a good performance and lay on the verbal and physical praise. Get down and hug the beast! He needs it. End the session with a little playtime. Do this every time and you'll be rewarded with a dog that looks forward to training sessions with enthusiasm. Obedience training can be useful and enjoyable to police and civilians alike. I see no reason why the police dog can't attend an AKC obedience class with other dogs and civilians. If you're starting a K-9 unit with only one dog, this will give him the opportunity to rub elbows with other dogs and handlers. This can be very helpful towards his socialization. Remember, OB and socialization can be done together. The other dog owners you meet might also be good prospects for decoys when Fido graduates to the bitework. These folks are already "bitten" by the training bug. Sometimes people are honored to do it. Some others put it in the same class as jumping out of perfectly good airplanes.

I made many mistakes in training and on the street. They are detailed throughout this book so that you might be better prepared than I was and

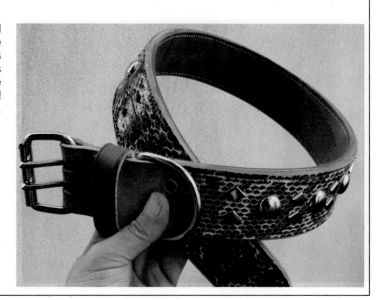

The current world champion Dogue De Bordeaux wears this collar, which was handcrafted by the author. 29-inch neck! Lotta dog, Lotta dog.

so that you will be exposed to less risk than I was.

How are you going to know when your dog is ready to graduate from obedience? If you are in a class, you will be given a diploma of some kind. If you do it on your own, your dog should hold a "down/stay" for five minutes with you out of sight. He should hold a "down/stay" with other people and dogs in his area for five minutes. He should walk quietly through crowds of people and other dogs on lead. He should of course do all turns, a perfect "heel," automatic "sit" at each halt on and off lead and respond perfectly to all verbal and hand signals. Don't even think about bitework until he graduates OB.

BITEWORK BEFORE OB?

One of the finest trainers I've had the pleasure of working

Considered the granddaddy of the American Bulldog, this is John D. Johnson and his boy "Elrod." Tip: don't slap John.

with is Sgt. Bob Anderson of the Palm Beach County Sheriff's Office and when he talks, I listen. (He speaks dog fluently.) He told me that he is only doing very basic OB with the dogs before taking them to the bitework. The reason is to build their confidence and to make them less introverted. By the time they start the bitework, they are fully aware of who the boss is. They just aren't required to be letter perfect. He is putting the polish on their OB after the bitework is completed because sometimes that final polish requires some forehead to forehead discussions with the dogs. These discussions can leave the dog a little confused or intimidated. By going through the bitework first, the dogs and handlers have more time to bond, hence fewer corrections are required when the final polish is done on the obedience field. Bob tells me he has done the last five classes in this manner and that it takes less time and trauma. When I asked where he learned of it, he shamelessly admitted to getting the idea from a child psychology book. Perhaps now the reader is beginning to understand why I'm only a student to dog training. Police K-9 has really caught on in recent years, as has the Schutzhund game. Dogs are being trained all over the U.S. now and in Europe especially. New techniques are being perfected daily. I'm still learning. I'm not surprised or embarrassed about it because

Kyle Symmes and "Woody." Kyle also owns "Chance" of *Homeward Bound* fame.

I'm too busy writing them down, and trying them. I remember just a few years ago some trainers wouldn't talk about their training techniques. They were closely guarded secrets. Well, I think those days are happily behind us for the most part. There's too many people training dogs now to maintain any secrecy. Many of these new techniques have been passed on by Sgt. Anderson and Sgt. Ron Shunk of the Belle Glade Police Dept. in Belle Glade, Florida.

ATTITUDE ADJUSTMENTS

WARNING...SOME OF THE FOLLOWING TECHNIQUES MAY OFFEND THE FINER SENSIBILITIES OF SOME OF THE DOG-SHOW CROWD AND "OLD YELLER" FANS MAY FAINT DEAD AWAY, BUT THESE TECHNIQUES MAY VERY WELL PREVENT A TRAGEDY IN YOUR FUTURE. "LASSIE" WILL FORGIVE ME...

OK, most of the foregoing dealt with when you do this, your dog should do that. I'm well aware that he doesn't always comply. Sometimes it's out of stubbornness and sometimes it's because he wants to dominate you. The dominance problem is almost always associated with a mature dog and a green handler. Let's say the new handler is taking his new charge over some hurdles. The dog does a few but really doesn't care for them. He lets the handler know his

word *"NO"* at full throttle, administered a vicious neck–breaker of a correction. That will generally straighten things out and establish the pecking order.

If it didn't and he repeats or escalates the challenge, now it is time. With the same firm two-hand hold (way up on the leash) raise the leash high enough into the air that Fido's back feet

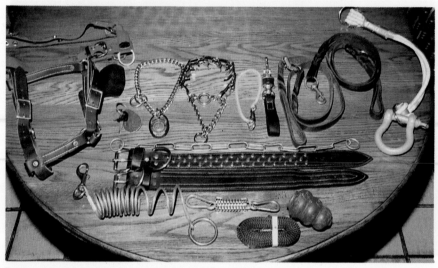

Some of the equipment used in protection training.

feelings with a growl. At the next session he does one hurdle, then stops and nips the handler. Uh-Oh! This clearly shouldn't have happened. It is the fault of the handler and if a professional trainer is running the class, it is his fault. At the first session the dog growled at the handler—a clear challenge of authority—and nothing was done. At that first growl the handler should have gotten a firm two-handed grip on the leash and while booming the

clear the ground and continue to hold him aloft until his efforts to escape are considerably diminished. That is not to say to the point of rigor mortis, but when you can see the fight is starting to ebb, lower him to the ground. If he is too heavy or you are too short, it won't work. In that case you give him a helicopter ride at the end of the leash until centrifugal force makes his feet leave the ground. About seven to ten revolutions usually does the trick and he'll generally crash land when you stop. If this sounds a bit harsh, I'm sorry. Anything short of this will be ineffective and you will cast in cement his desire to dominate over you. Translated it means roughly that his bad behavior will continue and he will be the boss—a very bad situation. He hasn't the brains for a management job and you couldn't live on his pay. He could also damage you severely the next time. Don't let a next time happen. Correct it immediately! The helicopter ride is the easier and safer of the two techniques. He is also defenseless against it. It is necessary. Once he knows you are the boss, he will never challenge you again and won't break a heel command to chase a cat into traffic. By administering the "attitude

The prong collar. These collars are especially effective on larger, tougher dogs such as those trained for protection and police work. Although this type of collar looks rather painful, it actually isn't because the skin around a dog's neck is not very sensitive.

adjustment" today, you may save his life tomorrow.

During all phases of OB a heavy welded choke is worn by your dog. If you do a helicopter ride while he's in a leather collar he might slip out of it and go through the windshield of your car.

If you are truly faint of heart and think I'm a barbarian because of what you just read, go to a riding stable some time and ask what the cure is for a recalcitrant horse. It makes our method pale by comparison.

Horses are big, dumb, heavy and strong. Allowed to have their own way they could cripple or kill you. If they can't be made to obey, they go to the glue factory. Dogs have sharp teeth and strong jaws. They can kill horses. Uncontrollable dogs become fertilizer. So which is more barbaric? Giving the dog a helicopter ride and getting his attention, or having him destroyed after he makes a gelding out of you? Take a deep breath and do what's necessary.

Son Brent holding a rattlesnake skin collar made by his dad for *Homeward Bound's* "Chance."

Agility

Running the swinging bridge.

The dog must get used to various obstacles and learn how to safely negotiate them so that he'll be confident when confronted by obstacles on the street. Sometimes he may have to chase someone through a furniture store, warehouse, factory, plowed field, alley, car lot or just about anything else you can think of. He will encounter every known surface in his travels including steel grates, slippery terrazzo floors, etc., which can make him hesitate or completely refuse to continue the pursuit. I've seen it happen. An obstacle course must be built or borrowed. The first obstacles you will need are hurdles. Six are required in USPCA competition (36 inches high), consisting of a picket fence, simulated hedge, brick wall, chain link, block wall and window. All of these can be purchased out of catalogues. The next obstacle is a broad jump consisting of six 1-inch-by-6-inch planks 6 inches off the

This is "Yeager," of True Grit Bullmastiffs, working out on a playground set. Imagine arriving at a riot with this guy!

Author's American Bulldog bitch, "Patch," negotiating the police agility course. Hurdles; broad jump; A-frame. No sweat.

ground adjustable from 6 to 10 feet in length. Next is a tunnel consisting of a culvert pipe 20 inches in diameter, 15 feet long. The dog must crawl through it. Next is an A-frame at least 6 feet high for toning the dog's hip muscles. The dog should go up and over 10 to 20 times, depending on its condition. Next is the "catwalk" consisting of a 6-foot-high ladder climb to a 16-inch-wide, 8-foot-long catwalk with a 45-degree ramp to exit. The dog must scale a six foot wall. Stacked barrels are also good but not mandatory.

Pit Bull "Rock" doing agility course, to include 6-foot vertical wall. He weighs 90 pounds.

SAFETY

The "O" course is potentially dangerous for your dog so care must be taken that he not be injured or frightened by it. Spot him! Start him jumping small hurdles like the 20-inch culvert. Allow him time to realize he can jump things and gain confidence. Praise him highly, making it a game if possible or at least fun. Don't *ever* drag him over a high hurdle. He'll be bruised and frightened and you will need two to three extra weeks to get him over his newfound fear. On the first several ladder attempts, spot him very closely and be *certain* he doesn't fall. You may also have to place his back feet. Do not let him get hurt on this or he may never do it again. Never let him chicken out and jump off (same reason). Remember, lots of praise. Careful not to give him too much help on the six-foot wall. He could develop a habit of making you shove him over the top. That is unacceptable in USPCA competition. An assistant pulling gently on a leash can be helpful at the ladder. Repetition is the key to success on the "O" course. The ladder will be the toughest. Baby talk and praise are what will work—coercion will not. Stay cool, give lots of praise and make it fun.

Above: American Bulldog Patch clearing the broad jump. Dogs that are to be used in police work must negotiate several types of terrain and be capable of jumping various objects. **Below left:** Author sending Patch over an A-frame. She lost a dewclaw on this poorly designed structure. **Center:** Jumping through a window hurdle. **Right:** This is the toughest and most dangerous obstacle on the police K-9 course. Use lots of praise and encouragement and don't let your dog chicken out or get hurt.

A K-9 German Shepherd floats over the picket fence.
Another receives a little added incentive at the broad jump from Bob Anderson with a light line on a prong collar.
Toning hip muscles on the A-frame.
Below left: Ascending the ladder. **Below right:** Waiting for a command at the top.

Above left: Launchpad view of an 8-foot broad jump. **Above right:** Deputy making sure his best friend doesn't fall. **Right:** Handler barking a "Hup" command, launches a recruit.

Patch obviously loves the obstacle course. After five trips over the top, she wants Mike to chase her. Fat chance.

The 7-foot A frame is good for toning the dog's hip muscles.

Patch clearing the window obstacle.

Scaling the 6-foot wall. This skill comes in handy when in pursuit of a running criminal.

Patch atop the catwalk.

Clearing the tunnel.

Patch making her way over stacked barrels. Another frequent occurrence for a police dog in hot pursuit.

Search

Patch looking for the author with the wind at her back. She's doing well. Lance Jackson with her.

There are four different types of search: tracking, area search, building search and article search.

TRACKING

Tracking is used to find lost people who have left the scene. Sometimes they are criminals, sometimes they are not. As all animals (humans included) go about their lives, skin cells are dying and constantly being replaced. In the case of humans those dead cells are mixed with sweat and all kinds of artificial fragrances, such as body lotion, deodorant, perfume or hair spray. When a skin cell dies and falls away it contains two substances that are detectable to the dog's nose. The first is an oil called sebum, which is produced by our hair follicles. Its job is to keep the skin soft and supple. The second and stronger of the two is bytiric acid. It is known to be the attracting agent and the sebum is known as the discriminating agent. The dog can identify you from all other human scents— sort of an olfactory fingerprinting system. Believe me, it works.

The dog is introduced to his first track by finding his master. The handler plays with the dog and gets him excited. He then puts a leash on him and hands the leash to an assistant known to the dog. The handler runs away from his dog, all the time calling to him to come. (The tone should indicate an invitation to play.) This of course gets him more excited. The handler now runs off and goes around a corner, actually a simple hide. The assistant waits long enough for you to get in your hide. He then starts the dog, who is brimming with curiosity and wants to catch up with you. He is allowed to run to where he last saw you. At this point, he is not allowed to go forward until he puts his nose down. He may very well do it naturally or the assistant can point to where you

left a personal item like a comb or wallet. From that point there should be a very heavy track that you made by shuffling your feet and maybe even lying down on the track several times. The idea here is to make a super-easy track for him so that he can't fail. It should also be no more than about 50 feet. When he finds you, make a very big deal of it. Three or four repetitions of this should suffice. He now knows his nose can be used to find things other than his food dish. When the assistant's finger pointed the way at ground level, Fido put his nose down to see what the finger was up to. When he did, guess who he smelled? The rest was as simple as following his nose. Tracks grow increasingly difficult and the dog soon becomes sharp. Equipment necessary for the task is as follows: a 15- to 30-foot tracking lead, a quality tracking harness, a willingness to get dirty and/or wet and a comfortable pair of shoes. You may early on notice Fido getting bored with tracking. There are two ways of supplying the necessary incentive to renew his enthusiasm. One is food laid on the track and at the end. This will work if he's a chow hound. The other incentive is giving him a bite as the reward. This works so well that you will notice a greater degree of difficulty getting him to out after a track. When they are made to work hard for the bite (a tough track), they seem to double their desire to hold on to the sleeve. Even the very best dogs will do this. It's as though they're saying, "You made me work for this, now you're gonna pay." It's almost like they're being poor sports about it.

German Shepherd Dog on track.

CROSS TRACKING OR SCENT DISCRIMINATION

At some time in training the trackers will encounter a situation where the track intersects track laid by another person. Sometimes the dog is following the smell of crushed vegetation and any track will smell the same to him. To avoid this, have the assistant leave a personal item at the beginning of the track such as a comb, brush, hat, shirt or glove. The dog will know what he is looking for by getting a snootful of scent from the article. He will follow that scent even if it crosses another. You will have just taught him to discriminate between more than one scent. He will have done it by following the trail of dead skin cells that were sloughed off the person he was tracking.

In either type of tracking only give the track command once. When Fido's nose is on the ground, move forward. When his nose comes off the ground, stop. This will teach him that if he wants to move forward, he must keep a deep nose. This also ensures that he doesn't miss a turn in the track. You of course were careful to have the assistant lay the track with the wind at his back. This will ensure that there will be no airborne scent. He will find it only on the ground. Praise is in order when his nose is down and you're moving forward. Not so much that you distract him, but just so he knows he's doing the right thing. When he's close to the hidden man, he will raise his head and stop, trying to locate the man visually. A verbal warning will usually produce a surrender. If it doesn't, release the dog.

AREA SEARCH

This differs from tracking in several ways. The dog finds scent particles in the air instead of on the ground. This method is quicker, and it can be done on- or off-lead depending on your particular circumstances. Area searches are done facing into the wind. The airborne scent forms a scent cone if the air is moving. The smallest and most concentrated part of the cone is just a few feet behind the man. The scent disperses as it blows further from the man, in the same fashion as diesel exhaust behind a bus. The best method to use is a grid pattern.

Wind velocity affects the scent cone in the following manner: higher wind speed results in a narrower scent cone, though stronger and more concentrated, a lower wind speed results in wider scent cones with a weaker scent.

The ideal area search is a wide open area with a 20 m.p.h.. breeze blowing steadily in one direction. Ambient temperature should be between 40 and 50 degrees. Steady wind means not having to reposition the dog because of wind shift. With no wind you will have to attempt a track, but this is only possible if you have a starting point where a suspect was last seen. An ideal tracking surface is in ankle-to-knee-high grass that is wet from dew. Scent will collect on the grass and stick to it because it is damp. The cool temperature will prevent it from evaporating. Flat surfaces allow a scent to be blown away, and blacktop is a poor surface because it's oil based, which is strong enough to mask scent. So, the worst possible scenario would be a hot

Tracking diagram

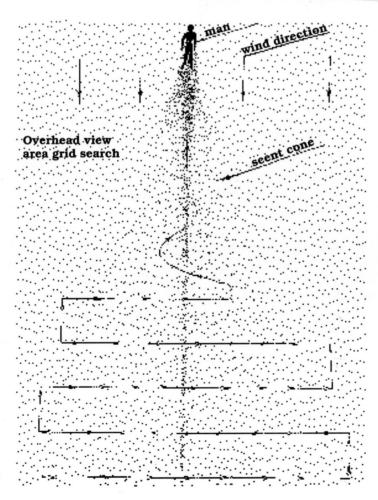

man

wind direction

Overhead view
area grid search

scent cone

Dog
Starts
Here

windy day tracking on blacktop. I wouldn't even start it. The best conditions will always be at night because the cooler temperatures will keep the dog from tiring and prevent evaporation of scent.

When training to track, expose your dog to all different types of areas and terrain; you never know where you're going to need him so let him experience as much as possible.

When tracking around irregular surfaces or around structures some confusing things will happen. Your dog may pull you along a wall where you know your assistant did not walk. Trust the dog. If his nose is on the ground, he's on the scent. The scent has just been blown off course a little by the wind. It may have piled up against a wall like snow. He may even try to climb a wall where the scent has piled up. He may not take a straight path but he'll find his man.

A good deal of controversy exists as to which breed is the best for tracking men. Bloodhounds will do longer and older tracks. It's my opinion that this is true because of the more relaxed temperament of the hound and his more sensitive nose. He doesn't have to work as hard to detect the scent, therefore he has more energy to devote to the trail. Any of the (protection) breeds will track quietly as opposed to the baying of the hound. When the bad guy hears the dog coming, his casual walk becomes a cross-country foot race. Of course if he sees your Shepherd or Rottweiler coming, he'll also feel the need to flee swiftly but then you can drop the leash and let your dog do what he's good at. I know of no Bloodhound that will bite. Where he will excel is in search and rescue work. Manhunting should be left to the breeds that are certifiable man–stoppers.

BUILDING SEARCH

The building search is potentially the most dangerous task the K-9 team will be called on to do. Teaching it is relatively simple, assuming the dog is already proficient at area search. It is basically the same thing except it is conducted indoors. Generally there is no wind inside a building but the air does move. Did you know that buildings breathe? They do. Some inhale, some exhale, depending on the heating or air conditioning systems.

There is an advantage to the building search in that almost none of the scent is blown away. The longer a man remains inside a building, the easier he is to find because more scent is distributed. To start the dog on

A really tenacious tracker will do whatever it takes to find his subject. **Top left:** Lift off! **Top right:** Scaling the tree. **Bottom left:** Way up in the branches, about 14 feet off the ground. **Bottom right:** Coming back to earth.

his first building search, an agitator is employed just outside the entrance to your chosen building. He fires up the dog, turns and runs into the building with the dog close on his heels. The dog catches him just inside. This is repeated several times with the man going progressively deeper into the building so that the dog learns it's OK to catch the bad guy inside. Eventually the bad guy does a simple hide (such as behind a door). The handler commands the dog to "find," just as he would in an open-area search. Fido will have to search the bad guy out before he can bite him. Gradually the hides become tougher and Fido gets better and better.

One thing I believe in is yelling a warning into the building before commencing your search. One real good reason is in case a cleaning crew is in the building. You should always check outside for work vans at the front door with identifying advertisements on the van doors. Assuming you've done this, yell the warning "Police Dept. K-9 Unit! *Come Out Or Get Dog Bitten!*" I know of no state requirement or law that mandates this warning, but a defense attorney will attempt to play on the sense of fair play of the jury. They will try to implant the thought in the jury's minds that an unannounced K-9 search is unfair, illegal and about as morally justified as firing torpedoes at a hospital ship during peacetime!

The plus side of this is that the perpetrator might surrender without a fight or bite, thereby removing any bogus grounds for a lawsuit. Now the other reason for the warning—this is the one that will provide the incentive to always yell the warning. When our bad guy realizes he is not

Left: Police dog about to be let into building for a search exercise.
Below: Sniffing out the area.

alone in this building, he learns terror. His adrenal glands go into red alert. This produces an odor undetectable to us but it's like lights and sirens for the dog. This makes the bad guy so easy to find, it's almost criminal. After a very few minutes (it seems like an eternity in hell to our bad guy), Fido locates him and bites him. In the opinion of this writer, this provides him with unparalleled incentives to seek out new avenues for making a living. The corrections system can not in five years equal the learning experience that a capable dog can provide in four minutes.

In a recent lawsuit filed against the West Palm Beach Police, a subject committed burglary and left before the arrival of a K-9. He was tracked to a hiding place and bitten when he refused to come out following a warning. His suit alleged that his civil rights were violated in that he was punished without benefit of trial. Unbelievable? It happened. He lost, but it goes to show you there's apparently no extreme too ridiculous for one of these vermin to go to in their attempt to circumvent earning a living.

BUILDING SEARCH TIPS

Once we have the dogs doing really well in bite work, we start playing hide and seek in earnest. The hides should become more difficult until we're really making him earn his money. In the real world scared burglars will hide in the damndest places.

Finding and apprehending the suspect, K-9 style.

Some of the hides are really good. Some aren't. Up inside false ceilings, chimneys, closets, ovens, clothes dryers, cabinets, shower stalls, etc. Trust your dog! If he's telling you the man is there, he's there. Just because he's not visible doesn't mean he's not there.

The most frustrating search of my career was in training one night. We were doing it in an elementary school. My dog alerted on an upright metal cabinet big enough to hide two big men in a standing position. The dog was too "stupid" to notice a big typewriter on a heavy metal table was pushed up against the double doors of the cabinet. He was obviously unaware that you couldn't get in the cabinet, close the doors, then push the typewriter up against the doors. I dragged him away from the cabinet three times before the man inside yelled and came out, flattened me and attempted to run away with Nick on his arm. He said he was unable to keep from laughing for much longer. Then he showed me how he got in the cabinet, closed the doors halfway while sticking his finger out the door to hook the underside of the table and drew it toward him as he shut the door. The table lacked only one inch of being flush against those doors. On the way out, the man was laughing so hard he couldn't walk as he was repeating the four-letter words I had called my "stupid" dog.

Rock's baby picture. He started tracking at a young age.

BUILDING SEARCH SAFETY TIPS

When doing building searches it is usually dark so as to imitate a real-life scenario. Of course there is a slight increase in risk because you could trip, slip or step on a rake or clothesline yourself. Conversely it adds a little extra tingle for the decoy too. He is, after all, in a darkened building trying to avoid detection by a 90-pound hairy brute with sharp teeth bent on his destruction. It would behoove the said decoy to make his hide so as to allow Sparky only one avenue of entrance to close on him. Roughly translated: don't be facing east when Sparky arrives out of the west. This could allow him to put a hitch in your gittalong. An easy way for the decoy to guarantee the safety of his cheeks is to wedge them firmly into a corner. This way he has an attack area that spans only 90 degrees instead of 360 degrees.

Another really good tip for a decoy is to be in a crouch or on his knees. This will narrow the attack area vertically. This can prevent the dog from crunching your crotch as you protect your face. In a lighted room this is not as important, but looking for a running Rottweiler in a black room while standing in the middle of it is a situation not to be envied. Let common sense and pain be your guide.

While giving safety tips I suppose I should mention a few things about running apprehension work. Work up to it slowly. Do the dog's first ten bites on lead in case he's targeting unprotected areas of the body. Nothing will increase your pucker factor quite like your first swordfight with a dog. That's when the dog is pushing the sleeve away to get to your unblemished hide. Instead of catching the dog on the sleeve you wind up defending yourself with it. It only happened to me once, but it took a week before my neck hairs would lie down again. My only scars are from that incident.

The dog in question was a smallish Rottweiler named Baby. He was owned by Doug Madigan, a civilian who trained a lot of police dogs in South Florida. The hardness of Baby's bite left nothing to be desired. In fact, he nearly broke my arm during my introduction to the hidden sleeve. Baby had hurt many decoys, mostly on running apprehensions. If you stumbled and the sleeve wasn't handy at the precise moment of impact, no problem. Baby would be just as happy lifting your cranial cap. We eventually took to drawing straws to see who would catch Baby. He seemed to get more ruthless and less forgiving each time out. So, one night after watching every man on the field refuse to catch him, I volunteered. Putting my arm deep into the sleeve, I started downfield at a trot. I was thinking no sweat, he's just another dog. I've caught plenty of dogs, Rottweilers included, even Bullmastiffs. I covered about 50 yards when I heard Doug say "Gittem!" I covered maybe another 15 yards when I heard it. It was a deep base thudding sound. The

pitter patter of little feet it wasn't. It was the typical Rottweiler loping gait and it was closing in on me. Each time those big front feet came down, he made a sound somewhere between a cough and a growl. I turned my head for a "Baby progress check." The overhead lights that illuminated the back side of the college campus were suddenly blocked out and I was in a shadow. Guess whose? I ducked, felt hot breath on my right ear and felt him run across my right shoulder. I watched him turn 180 degrees in midair and land perfectly on all fours just long enough to go airborne at my face. I was still in a stumble and waving my arms trying to get my balance. Just a quick glance down his throat was all I needed before deciding to move my face quickly to the left. Both arms were still outstretched as though I was telling a fish story. His jaws snapped shut on my right bicep and the upper edge of the sleeve. It didn't hurt. Somehow I wiped him off with the forearm part of the sleeve. I could now hear more thuds in the grass and Doug screaming for all he was worth. The word *"OUT"* was falling on deaf ears. The dog launched himself at me seven or eight more times. Each time, he pushed the sleeve away trying for leg, crotch, torso and face but wanted nothing to do with that sleeve. Doug finally got there, got him by the collar and literally dragged him away. He was tearing up clods of sod as he went. You could have taken my pulse on my forehead. The other handlers and

I just stood there staring at each other in disbelief for a minute.

To my knowledge, that was the last time Baby was ever allowed to do running apprehension work. I caught him a couple more times in building search scenarios utilizing the procedures described previously without mishap.

Now don't be discouraged and let that little story change your mind about training dogs. Dogs like Baby only come around every 300 years or so. The two small scars on my right bicep are the only ones I have after making hundreds of catches. I think if you exercise a little common sense and some of my safety tips, you can expect to live relatively scar-free, if not to a ripe old age. Decoy work is probably safer than driving on the freeway. I don't want you to think, though, that catching dogs in running apprehension work is totally without risk.

ARTICLE SEARCH

This is very easy to teach. It is a continuation of the fetch game. It should be done in exactly the same manner as an area grid search (facing into the wind). Start with fairly large, easy-to-pick-up objects that hold scent well. A glove is perfect. Wear it for five minutes or just blow into it prior to the search and it will be loaded with scent. Hopefully you were playing fetch with your dog and using a verbal command such as "fetch" or "git it" or whatever. If not, start. When he arrives at the toy and mouths it or picks it up, crouch and slap your thighs. Now using a voice dripping with sugar, call him to you with a one-syllable word. I like the word "bring" Short, to the point and it can't be confused with any other command. If he doesn't come right away, keep trying. Don't ever lose your temper in this exercise. The dog must do the article search because it's fun. It's an extension of his fetch game. If he doesn't catch onto coming to you right away, run from him. He loves a footrace. He'll come running. As soon as he's near you, praise him and coax him in close so you can get a hand on his collar. This accomplished, give the command "bring" and take the article out of his mouth and say "Good Boy!" (A hug is appropriate here. He has to have a reason to bring the articles to you. Verbal praise and hugs are a good reason.) Making him sit when he arrives with the article is a good idea. It is a stay command of sorts and can prevent him from running when you reach for the article. *Never* chase him to get the article. This will start a game of keep-away, which is hard to break. Dogs love this game because they know you can never catch them. Do the exercise every day for five or ten minutes. At the end of two weeks, he'll have the routine down pretty solid. Now cut the glove in half. Attach keys to it, continue another week, and cut it in half again. In two or three days cut it down some more. The idea is to get him used to the nasty metal keys in his mouth. Eventually bare keys will pose no problem. Start using new articles such as credit cards, junk jewelry, pocket knives and eventually a handgun, yes a handgun. Any old relic out of the armory or property room will do. Be sure to scent up the new articles each time by rubbing them on your person for a minute before the toss. Later, when he gets better, you can skip this step.

Eventually graduate to tossing the articles out of the dog's immediate sight so he'll have to use his nose. Use the same area for a while and always use the command "fetch" or whatever you like, as long as it's one syllable. Always use the command "bring." After a couple of months these two words are programmed into his brain. Fetch means "it's out there." Just because he didn't see the toss, doesn't mean it's not out there. Never get cute and tell him to fetch when there's nothing out there. Need I explain? Of course not. Always praise him when he "brings." Remember that he's doing it for praise and because it's fun. The size of the article should gradually shrink, and the number should increase. Just make sure there is an article for every fetch command. He can eventually get so good that retrieving .22 shell casings won't be too difficult. Ten minutes every day—it's that simple. I've seen some dogs bring back dimes. Police dogs will possibly be called upon to find lost evidence on a track, such as murder weapons, holdup money or narcotics (buried or otherwise). Let article search be the playtime after a hard day's work.

Whatever in the world would a personal protection dog need of this training? Let's say you're in your yard or on the high school campus throwing a football with your son. He goes long and you uncork the bomb. With it goes the $10,000 diamond pinky ring your wife just gave you for your birthday! If your dog can't article search, the ring is lost. If you've taken ten minutes a day with him, he will find it and drop it in your hand. Valuable dog or what?

Once again, the dog gets his man. Too bad this was only an exercise.

Bitework

American Bulldog Terminator, SchH.W.H. titled, displaying the rippling power that puts this breed at the top of the heap. Bred by Sure Grip kennels.

This is the most interesting and important phase. If the dog won't bite, he is useless as a protection dog or a police dog. He must display a certain amount of courage or he will never hold his ground against an aggressor. He must protect his handler, car, home or whatever needs protecting. If he is nervous, skittish or shy, he just won't do. If his teeth and gums aren't healthy, he will soon lose his desire to bite even if he has plenty of courage. Pain will eventually train him not to bite.

This phase is also the most controversial area of training in that everyone has an opinion as to what methods are the best. In reality no method is the best. All dogs are as unique as humans. They have nearly as many quirks as we do and will all respond to the various training techniques; however, sometimes a dog won't pick up on what you're teaching. Alternate methods are then called for. If you don't know them because you're under the impression only one method will do, then you will be out of luck. Remember, there is no golden rule in dog training. What worked on your dog, may not work on mine.

NECESSARY EQUIPMENT
1. Tie out—chain, cable, rope or nylon strap
2. Heavy duty agitation harness
3. Heavy duty agitation leash
4. Spring, shock cord, lunge line or chain-link fence
5. A place to anchor spring, shock cord, lunge line or chain-

Bite suits teach dogs to bite anywhere. It prevents dogs from becoming sleeve happy. John in the suit. Preacher and Patch on the suit. These three have been on TV with this act.

link fence

   6. One or more assistants

   7. Burlap sack

   8. Privacy—a park is not the place for agitation. You don't have the time to answer questions from all the nosy passersby. Most people will only think the wrong things anyway.

TESTING CANDIDATE DOGS

   This is yet another area where opinions abound. Though an avid admirer of Bill Koehler, I think his test of gunfire is a bit severe. It will certainly produce a hard dog...eventually. Unfortunately it will bypass dogs that appear marginal, but will make great dogs in time. It is as follows: the candidate dog is walked past a hideout; a bad guy then pops out screaming and fires a

Some of the necessary leather. The collar and harness were made by the author.

couple shots into the air; the dog that attempts to attack gets high marks. He damn well should. That's a tough test! Dogs holding their ground are

on new ground on lead with his owner. Wearing some type of outrageous outfit helps to get the attention of even the most naive dog. Example: weird hat,

Some of the equipment needed to train dogs for protection and police work.

worthy of further tests. OK, it is a valid test, but it is my opinion that you will go through many dogs before finding one that makes the grade.

I prefer to introduce gunfire later and gradually so that the dog can get used to it without winding up looking like Bill the Cat of "Bloom County" fame. Gunfire shakes me up at the breakfast table, and I'm fearless. At the target range it's not a big deal. Everything has its place.

I prefer putting the candidate

trenchcoat, swim fins or big galoshes, shorts and big chrome sunglasses. Remember, arousing the dog's suspicion is our purpose. Something is definitely different about this guy and watching him closely should be foremost on the dog's mind. A real sneaky, slithering approach is done and if it doesn't elicit concern on the dog's part, I give him the necessary incentive to watch me more closely.

Remember many candidate dogs have led very sheltered

lives and may still be very naive. A light switch appears and a big show is made with it before you give him a zinger

across the front legs. If he cowers or whimpers, he's out. If he holds his ground and appears fascinated, continue. If he growls or barks, he's looking good. If he attacks, he has a new home. Let the gunfire come later and preferably from a distance, start with firecrackers to blanks to real gunfire at a target range. Here he can learn by watching you and friends to be relaxed with it. Every dog I've ever owned went shooting with me often and I've never had one who wasn't cool as a cucumber around the range. They accept it as normal in short order. If your dog has turned his back on you (the agitator) it's easy to teach him not to trust you being behind him. He's left his butt open to attack, so attack it. Pull his tail, grab the loose skin on his flank. This should get his attention. If it doesn't, look elsewhere. It has been my experience that this will produce more good dogs. The gunfire method will definitely show you if the dog is hard and ready to

Agitator Steve Baccari with 100-pound bulldog Giants Diesel of Land of Giants. Owner and trainer, Ken Buzzell.

Can you see why Mike Harlow loves this dog? This is only two weeks into bitework.

go right now. I prefer another method. It doesn't even require a gun. I'm talking about the hard stare. The hard stare is what happens just before a dogfight and a dogfight is exactly what I'm trying to provoke. Really tough dogs will light up with just a stare. Mine did at the age of four months. The agitator was a very petite woman who was *seated* at the time! Needless to say, I was pleased with that dog and still have her.

Providing our recruit with a reason to pay closer attention to the advance of the agitator is important. It is equally important that it be done properly. A screaming frontal attack and a switch in the face is wrong because all you want at this point is for the recruit to be alert. Teach him that just by staying alert he can avoid the switch. The agitator should also be a chicken-hearted coward, easily frightened away simply by the dog's alerting. A growl or a bark will be icing on the cake at this point, but isn't yet necessary. Also, you're not testing his fighting ability; you're only seeing if he will fight. If striking him is necessary and it may very well be, stay away from his front. By stinging his butt you quickly teach him not to let you behind him. Good. You're arousing suspicion in him. The aggressor always acts in a suspicious manner, approaching with stealth. Furtive eye movement is a giveaway and should be part of the aggressor's arsenal of acting skills brought to bear. It telegraphs ill intent in both the human and the canine world. It makes a difference that you can see in the dog's reactions. If he whips around and stiffens upon your approach, shrink back a bit, like a vampire being shown a crucifix. The handler of course gives verbal encouragement— "good boy!" Now he knows you like it when he shows some backbone. If he growls or barks, run like hell. The handler will provide verbal and physical praise that will leave no doubt in the dog's mind that he has done well. If he makes a maximum effort to rid the earth of your shadow, you are no longer looking at a candidate but at a new family member.

Left: Banuelos' Predator doing a credible job in a Schutzhund bark and hold exercise. He is the first AB to earn a SchH.III title. **Bottom left:** Predator. **Bottom right:** Predator's son Ike, SchH.III.

If you test someone else's dog, don't forget to act sneaky on the approach and terrified if he alerts, growls or barks.

fights the dog. He should be acting, not just fighting. In the real world it is customary, when getting bitten, to grimace and

Mike Rider and a terrific Giant Schnauzer.

THE IMPORTANCE OF PROPER AGITATION

Agitation is without doubt the most important part of training for police K-9 or personal protection. Done wrong, it can ruin a good dog and get somebody hurt. Agitation done properly is a beautiful thing to watch. It is a learning process for the dog. The agitator actually programs the dog to react properly to different situations and threats. He teaches the dog when he can and can't bite. He teaches him certain types of people to be wary of and who to be relaxed with. If it's beginning to sound to you like the agitator is the teacher, you're catching on.

We place much importance on who teaches our children. We should do the same when it comes to our dogs. Stay away from the macho type who only

even scream and beg. Too many agitators adopt the backwards walking, woodsawing motion with the sleeve with no expression on their face or in their voice, if they're making any noise at all. Robot agitators don't teach the dog, they bore him by doing everything in a predictable pattern. People are emotional, especially when they're angry, frightened or in pain. The dog needs to learn this and he won't learn it from the robot agitator. Pick the agitator carefully. He isn't always the trainer, but he damn well is the teacher.

Reality is the key word here. All agitation and related scenarios should appear as they do in the real world. The dog is being trained to protect you from assaults by people. People become more aggressive in groups and some of the agitation should reflect that. Another courage booster is alcohol. Create scenarios with the smell of alcohol (not by showing up drunk). Walking through a puddle of beer should suffice. I suppose if you're really into it, you could pour a can over your head. The dog will thank you for it later.

STARTING AGITATION

The aggressor now becomes bolder. He gets closer and becomes increasingly difficult to scare away. The dog must work harder. He should now be lunging and snapping at our bad guy. If he does, the bad guy screams and runs away. This deserves tons of praise. The next day the aggressor returns to find the dog securely staked out on a shock cord, lunge line or stiff spring that is fastened to something solid. A chain-link fence will take the place of the shock-absorbing spring or shock cord. The idea is to soften the jolt of the dog coming to the end of the line. To further enhance this put your dog in a harness rather than in his collar. The object is to get the bad guy in as close as possible without getting him bitten. He must know exactly where the end of the dog's leash is. The guy is armed with a burlap rag or sack. A couple of sneaky passes are made. If the dog's reaction is strong, the guy runs away. This increases Fido's confidence. After a five-minute break we are again ready. The guy approaches as sneakily as possible, turns to run when Fido lights up but turns again and comes at the

Proper agitation is the key ingredient in bitework training. The agitator must be loud, emotional, and aggressive to simulate a real-world situation.

Agitator Steve Baccari with Giants
Black Sabbath, a 100-pound dog
owned by Lauren Goldman.

dog. He gets extremely close, with the rag held four to five inches out from his body in front of the dog. Now furious, the dog should grab the rag as soon as it's within reach. If he does, the bad guy screams and limps away as though mortally wounded. The handler lets the dog have the rag as a trophy if he wants it and gets down low and hugs the beast, all the time squealing, "Good boy!"— major, major victory! Your mutt just bit a bad guy, tore a large piece off him and sent him scurrying away screaming and limping; end of exercise. If he didn't take the rag but tried for the man, he is deserving of praise but the exercise must be repeated until the dog takes the rag. Biting the rag is the dog's reward for his hard work and is the key to releasing his frustrations. It may not happen in one day, so don't burn out the dog by repeated work with no victories. All the praise in the world won't work forever. He must eventually take the rag to release frustrations, to get his first bite, to get his first victory and to learn his first lesson: that he can stop the frustrating teasing of the bad guy by biting previous question, "Why burlap?"

FROM RAG TO SLEEVE

This next step is a relatively simple one. It is often unnecessary with a really tough, confident dog. The transition is accomplished by simply draping the rag over the arm that has been inserted into a lightly constructed puppy sleeve. When Fido bites the rag, he also gets the arm. After a few repeats, you can probably retire the rag for the remainder of his training. He'll actually prefer the sleeve

Rock's first bite. He was allowed to have the sleeve as a trophy.

him. It is then a whole new ball game. Absolute tons of praise are in order. Baby talk him all the way back to the car. No more work for today. End it on this fabulously good note.

After several successes with the rag over a period of several days it becomes time to graduate to the real thing, or as close to it as we dare go. We're talking about a padded protection sleeve made of jute. This material is very similar to the burlap sack, which should answer your because it doesn't immediately go limp when bitten. The agitator now starts a back and forth sawing motion with the sleeve. This results in a combination of good things. The movement excites the dog (arousing his prey drive) and makes it more difficult for him to hold on. Now he has to bite harder to avoid losing his grip and suffering the frustration and humiliation of watching the guy run away to safety. The agitator *must* run off to teach the dog this lesson. He must bite hard if he wants to hang on. A half-hearted bite won't work on the street and it shouldn't be allowed to work in training. There are documented cases of dogs being slung off by centrifugal force, sometimes because the bad guy was drunk or doped up and wasn't feeling the pain. Other times it is because the dog only got the coat-sleeve and not the arm within. This is the result of poor training.

Accept nothing less than a full-mouth bite from your dog. The reasons are as follows: more teeth holding lessens the chance of any teeth breaking. With all the teeth gripping, the dog is far less likely to pull the bite out, which would result in grievous bodily injury. Punctures, bruises and even broken bones heal. Ripped tendons and nerves do not. Front-mouth bites cause these types of injuries. Permanent or disfiguring injuries are the ones that shock the members of the grand jury. The back of the dog's mouth has a mechanical advantage due to the hinge being closer to the object, resulting in more leverage. More leverage equals a harder bite. A few minutes with a nutcracker will graphically illustrate the principle. It is common knowledge that the various bulldog breeds bite harder. The reason is twofold. Firstly, the muscles that close the jaws are well developed. Secondly, they have relatively short muzzles, which guarantees

Second day of bitework! She's already biting hard on the soft sleeve.

the object of the bite will be closer to the hinge or fulcrum where there is more leverage. More leverage equals a harder bite, every time. This is why bulldogs make such terrific catch dogs. They can't be slung off.

TEACHING THE BULLDOG BITE
The combination of the soft sleeve and the long wolflike fangs of the German Shepherd make hanging on pretty easy for this breed, which can encourage him into a soft or front mouth bite. If this is what's happening it's time to teach him the bulldog bite. This is accomplished by retiring the soft sleeve and graduating to a hard sleeve. Even if your dog is biting pretty hard, it is still smart to get him working a hard sleeve. It's going to toughen up even a good bite. As far as I'm concerned there's no such thing as too hard of a bite. Some sleeves are of the "bite bar" type. They have a bar of leather-covered bite area that protrudes

Land of Giants stud dog Giants Diesel at 5 years and 100 pounds showing a full mouth bite on the sleeve.

from the barrel of the sleeve between wrist and elbow. The best ones are "V-shaped" so that it is absolutely impossible for the dog to hold on. A dog doing a front-mouth bite will slip off the bite bar every time because he can't get his teeth into the harder surface and the shape of it is all wrong for holding. He will slip off repeatedly until he finally makes the connection that he can only hold on when his fangs go past the bite bar to the softer material behind it. Another small miracle happens when he does this. The bite bar winds up at the rear or hinge of his jaw. Remember, this is the "fulcrum" of the lever. This is where the most leverage is, and more leverage equals a harder bite.

The other kind of hard sleeve is a barrel sleeve with no bite bar at all. It is equally as impossible to hang onto with a front-mouth bite. Only a full-mouth bite will hold. There is no bite bar for the back teeth to grip, so this sleeve is made a little softer so that it will crush into its own bite bar. This is by far the most difficult sleeve for the dog to hold. It should be reserved for the advanced dog with a crusher bite. It will produce hard biters, which is exactly what we want. A super-hard biter causes nerve pinches, which often result in instant pain. This is the bulldog bite. The dog is now impossible to sling off, his teeth won't break and he won't shred our urban predator—a much better arrangement. I learned the lesson of the sleeves the hard way.

When I purchased my fully trained dog, he bit like an alligator. The demo that I watched was on a hard sleeve with a bite bar. Most of the jute was worn away from use, leaving a large exposed area of hard leather. It was very slippery, yet the dog held on even when swung in circles. The reason was the full-mouth bite. Here was a skinny 60-pound German Shepherd who was an absolute master of the bulldog bite. I was impressed and took him home. My trainer only used soft sleeves for reasons unknown to me. In about a month I had a dog that would only do a front-mouth bite, and a pretty poor one at that. My alligator was now a toy poodle with pink toenails. Use soft sleeves only for beginners. To develop a hard bite, get a hard sleeve.

Another disadvantage of a front-mouth bite is that sometimes the teeth will miss the meat and only get the clothing. When the clothing starts tearing away in long strips, it is hard for the dog to resist continuing this new sport. My dog depantsed a suspect one night and was content to shake his new trophy while the criminal ran away. I had to take the pants from him and send him after the now naked runner. At the second catch, there was no confusion about what to bite. Back to the drawing board and back to the hard sleeve.

Top and Middle: Novices take note. If the dog releases the sleeve, the decoy falls *away* from the dog. **Bottom:** Letting new dogs keep the sleeve builds their confidence. She wanted no part of it after the first time, when she realized nobody was in it.

TEACHING THE HOLD

Police work is quite different than Schutzhund competition. In police work there is a good chance of coming up against armed criminals. Not so in Schutzhund. In Schutzhund they teach something called the bark and hold. Basically, when the criminal stops fighting, the dog stops biting. Also if the dog locates an intruder, he only barks in the face of the intruder until help arrives or until the intruder moves. On the competition field, help arrives in

Steve Baccari taking the hit from Giants Diesel.

a matter of seconds. In real life, if your dog is barking in the face of an armed bad guy, it will probably be his last bark. If your dog "was" your only line of defense, you are now in big trouble. In the real world, it's better if your dog is holding the bad guy in his jaws until help arrives. This is yet another one of those lessons I learned the hard way. Another reason to leave the dog on the thug is because he may renew his efforts to escape. If the dog was outed, he will have to re-attack, which will make new puncture wounds. One set of punctures per customer looks much better than 15 re-bites (four punctures per set). We don't want to look overzealous out there when we have a protection-trained dog.

To teach the dog the hold is relatively simple. It is done in a completely realistic fashion by two simultaneous methods. First teach him that when he doesn't hold the bite, the guy escapes. Second, when the dog releases a bite, he is attacked by the guy. By re-biting, the attack stops, as it does in real life. It is nearly impossible to beat a dog that is clamped on your arm and shaking your fillings loose. Don't think so? Take the sleeve off and try it. If your dog utilizes the bark and hold on the street it will only work on unarmed men. The bite and hold works on almost everybody and is the only method I can recommend. It provides the most safety and the least liability (fewer holes). An argument can be made that in a

Giants Sasha, a red-nose APBT from Land of Giants kennel, taking her first bite.

building search you may lose sight of your dog and how are you going to find him if he's not barking? So far, the criminal has been very cooperative in helping me locate my dog.

SLEEVE-HAPPY DOGS

"Sleeve–happy" is a term used to describe a dog that has had too much of the same thing and is now programmed into a very narrow spectrum of performance. Every single time this dog was given a bite, he saw an aggressor wearing a huge protective sleeve. The sleeve made the aggressor look like a fiddler-crab. Over and over and over he attacked the man with the huge arm. Now in his first real situation, he closes the gap on a *real* bad guy. He quickly overtakes him just as in his

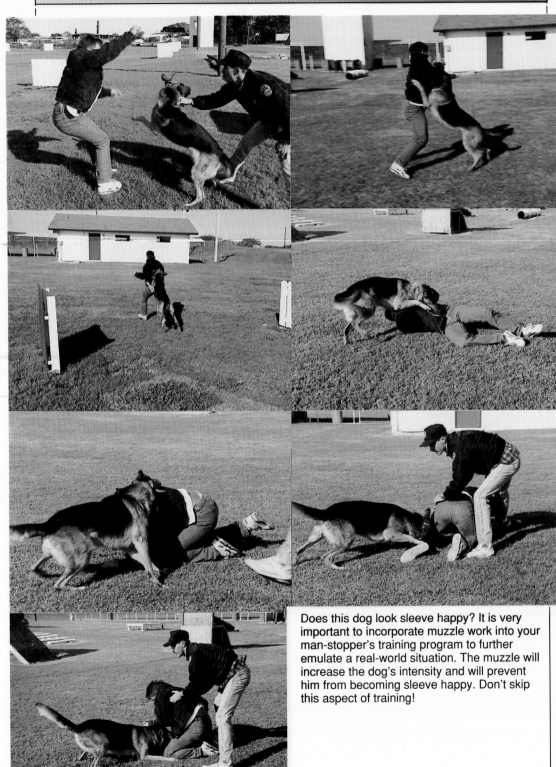

Does this dog look sleeve happy? It is very important to incorporate muzzle work into your man-stopper's training program to further emulate a real-world situation. The muzzle will increase the dog's intensity and will prevent him from becoming sleeve happy. Don't skip this aspect of training!

training scenarios, but upon arrival he notices something very different, something he has never before seen in his training. A bare arm! In his frustration of not being able to find the sleeve, he is now running circles around the man and not biting. In Schutzhund this is OK because the worst that will happen is that they will deduct points from your score. In the real world it can get him and you killed.

The answer is to train as realistically as possible. Bad guys don't wear big protection sleeves. Bad guys actually try to keep the dog from biting them because they're pretty sure it's going to hurt. Many times they will turn their backs on the dog and fold their arms to protect their hands. The answer is to train Fido to bite targets of opportunity, not just large arms. This is done by two methods: muzzles and bitesuits. The muzzle teaches him he can knock them down and wrestle with them without getting hurt. Many of the bad guys who surrendered without a fight told me later that they were pretty sure they could have won a fight against my dog, but were afraid I would have shot them as a result. I did nothing to dispel this myth, but I always offered them a chance to prove it—no takers.

I'm actually in serious doubt that a well-trained dog can be beaten in a fight against an unarmed man. I've done enough muzzle work to convince me

that a determined dog is very hard to beat even if he's muzzled. They are incredibly quick and learn very fast that your hands are the enemy. Muzzle work teaches them to counter any attempt to grab them by biting the offending hand. In a real fight, one bite on the hand is all that is necessary to take all the steam out of the bad guy. Muzzles also frustrate the dog because he can't get his teeth into the target. It usually results in a marked increase in his drive. When the muzzle comes off, his

A handler's eye view of what it looks like when your dog reacts to an aggressive human.

plan is to give you the "new look." The agitator will notice a harder bite, and outing him may be a little tougher.

Next we progress to the bite suit. Now that the decoy has

overall protection, he should purposely keep his arms out of the dog's reach. This frustrates the dog. If he wants to release his frustrations, he must take the bite where he can. If the decoy feeds Fido the arm, you have just wasted the price of the suit and your time. Suits cost a small fortune and are worth every penny. If the decoy is afraid to take a high chest bite, have the dog on lead. If the dog targets unprotected hands, feet or face, hide the decoy between boxes, tires, haybales or whatever so that the only exposed area is the target area: back, butt, chest, side or legs. He should be targeted on all these areas so that the dog feels comfortable biting anywhere, without hesitation. This type of training teaches him proper streetfight etiquette. This is what wins fights and wins them quickly. Winning quickly is important because he may be fighting more than one antagonist. A dog trained in this manner is heavily favored in a fight against a man. In a real fight, the handler should be right in the middle of it helping his dog and giving plenty of verbal encouragement. Together you are the irresistible force. You *will* win.

HIDDEN SLEEVES

Hidden sleeves are another tool in the trainer's arsenal of equipment, enabling the creation of realistic training scenarios. If the proper preliminary work has been done with the muzzle and bitesuit, the way of testing him outside of a real situation is with a hidden sleeve. It has no hinge or bite bar, nor very much padding. All this combines to make a sleeve very small in diameter that can be concealed inside a light coat or sweatshirt without the telltale bulge of the typical protection sleeve. It looks more like a bare arm to the dog, so we are able to test him before hitting the street and betting our lives on a dog that won't bite a bare arm. The United States Police Canine Association uses the hidden sleeve exclusively in their competitions. It's the only way of testing the dog short of a real bite situation. Remember, we want to avoid the fiddler-crab look and prevent the dog's brain from going into attack mode simply because he sees the huge arm. This is conditioned response. We want him responding to the man's aggressive behavior, not his oversized arm. Otherwise, he might attack the first innocent bodybuilder he sees.

Tom Bland's AB, Preacher, weighs 125 lbs. and hits like a freight train. He flattens the author effortlessly then drags him around the area. Though he enjoys wrecking him on the field, Mike Harlow is the only non-family member he lets in his house.

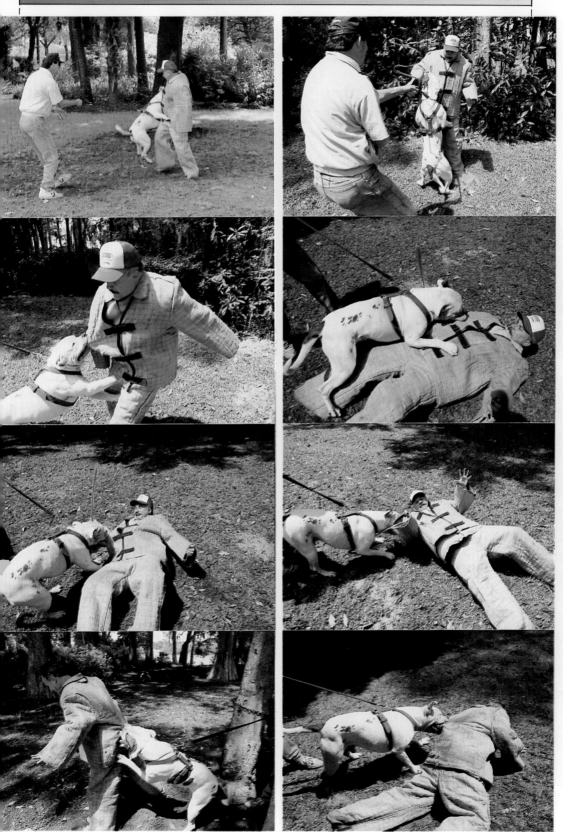

Norm Garner likes Malinois. He's teaching this one to snarl.

TECHNIQUE

Using the hidden sleeve can be a bit more risky. It doesn't cover the hand or the deltoid area of the arm. Some of them don't even cover the upper triceps if you're tall. It's not a sleeve for the novice decoy. The lack of padding can be painful if a wrist bite occurs. The ideal target area is the forearm and elbow, preferably the forearm. It has its own padding of muscle and will keep the bite pressure off your bones. Wrist bites are an invitation to nerve pinches.

Nerve tremors can simulate a powerful electric shock and bring you to your knees. Always catch him on the forearm.

REALISTIC SCENARIOS

When training a dog, one must remember that even though it is predictable to the handler and decoy, it is or should be a complete surprise to the dog. Each session should attempt to add a new twist so as not to burn out the dog or have him anticipate the decoy's next move. This is how decoys lose their sense of humor. Never hide in the same spot during building searches. You want him to use his nose, not his memory. Use hidden sleeves when possible. Realistic agitation is also important. A simulated escalating argument is a valuable training scenario (civil

This is Rock, an American Pit Bull Terrier, demonstrating the perfect full mouth bite. The hard bite is one phase of training that Rock never needed much instruction on. The leash is hooked up to a chain link fence, which makes a good shock absorber when agitating tough dogs. Notice a mask was put on to awaken his dormant distrust of sneaky strangers. It seemed to have worked rather well.

If this photo series looks painful, it is. That is a thin bite suit and a hard biter. This particular dog gets revved up when gunfire is introduced, an addition to the training session which further creates a realistic situation.

agitation). Don't forget crowd situations and fights with two or more antagonists. Your chances of being assaulted are much greater when they outnumber you, because in addition to there being safety in numbers, there is also courage in numbers and is directly related to the number of beers consumed. Create scenarios with simulated drunk bad guys. Spill some beer and have your decoys walk through it. Dogs need to learn extra caution with drunks due to their increased courage and decreased pain threshold. Feeling no pain isn't just a figure of speech. A person's loud, stumbling, arm-waving behavior generally intensifies the dog's suspicion, but the smell of alcohol should be the dog's "key" indicator to be on guard.

Beware of folks with canes and crutches. My dog never accepted my friend Pete, who gets around on crutches. He also went for a woman's face one night as she used her cane to point out the way the bad guys went. Luckily, he was on lead. He was just doing his job; he thought she was going to hit me with the cane. Her eyes opened wide with amazement and she pointed two more times with the cane, each time getting a similar response from the dog. This sort of thing will antagonize the dog.

Building searches are done in warehouses, garages, houses, stores, factories, etc. Every conceivable surface will be encountered so be sure to include the same when training. Some dogs become soft-mouthed when on unsure footing. If so, give them plenty of work on these surfaces. Want to do courage tests, or better yet, program him for invincibility? Blocks of styrofoam in packing boxes or the boxes themselves make great training bludgeons that won't injure Fido. Styrofoam popcorn is also great to throw at him and on the floor for weird but realistic warehouse footing.

PRECAUTIONS FOR AGITATORS AND TRAINERS

During all phases of protection training, a switch or light rod is

Steve Baccari taking a high hit from Giants Diesel.

useful for two purposes only:

1. To increase the dog's frustration level with threats and mild stings.

2. To teach the dog that he is invincible and insensitive to the pain offered by a stick-wielding antagonist.

what the dog will do while receiving the beating that a *real* bad guy would give him. Remember, if you will, that a *real* bad guy won't be wearing a sleeve and with a *real* dog clamped on his arm, I have some *real* doubts as to his commitment to the fight

Imagine you're a professional purse snatcher and just spotted one in this station wagon. This sequence of photos might give you the necessary inspiration to change your job description, don't you think?

Using the switch or light rod for a courage test is stupid and could result in ruining a perfectly good dog. Anyone attempting to beat the dust out of a dog to see what he's got should in the interest of realism conduct the test without a sleeve! That is reality. The excuse given most often for this is to see

or his ability to beat the hair off the dog, don't you? He will experience nerve tremors that will make him think he took a bath with a toaster. Having been bitten both with and without a sleeve, I can tell you that a courage test of the type described would be stupid, unfair, unrealistic and

Blackwell's Ida Red.

could train a good dog to run from a stick. Instead, program Fido with that stick.

PROGRAMMING FOR INVINCIBILITY

This is a certain type of training that all police and protection dogs should experience, but not all of them do. It is unwise to attempt to beat a dog off a sleeve. Do just the opposite. Make a big show of swinging the stick, but contact him only lightly so as to make him think he can take any amount of punishment imaginable and keep right on fighting. If you're feeling a little guilty about hiding the real truth from your best friend, don't despair. The reason for this deceit is that you want him to fly into action when reacting to a threat. No hesitation. When the bad guy raises a fist or knife or club or even a gun, hesitation is unacceptable. By allowing your dog to win every single contest in training, you are programming him into thinking that he is not only invincible, he's immortal!

RUNNING APPREHENSIONS

Probably the most important thing for the prospective decoy to remember is proper presentation of the sleeve. It must be an easier target than the rest of your anatomy, if you wish it to remain intact. The dog has for the most part been fed the sleeve up to now and he is programmed to take it because it is what he's used to. If you don't hide it from him, he will probably oblige you by taking the familiar sleeve. Safety and common sense demand that you hold the sleeve well out from your body in a horizontal manner. This is called targeting the sleeve. It is obviously the easiest target for the dog so he will take it. You will in fact ensure it by looking back over your shoulder and watching his approach. If he's going to the wrong side or going for a leg, you might want to turn around and feed him the sleeve. If you weren't looking, you will probably look the next time. The dog will provide you with a reminder to pay closer attention to him. Just one of these

Blackwell's Polar Bear

reminders could make you a little apprehensive. It could also be rough on your wardrobe, so don't do your decoy duties in a rented tux or police uniform.

Aside from getting a uniform shredded, it could set a bad example for the dog. If he is not allowed to bite a uniform in training, he might not do it accidentally on the street in the heat of battle such as in a riot or bar-fight. My dog Nick bit a cop one night when he, another officer and I were trying to break up a group of teenage boys who were in a running slugfest in the middle of the street. Nick was airborne and homing in on a tasty rear end when Dennis stepped between Nick and lunch. Dennis became lunch. I guess Nick recognized him at the last second. He just gave Dennis a good pinch for getting in the way. If they weren't close friends, it might have been worse. Dennis decoyed for us more than anyone else and babysat Nick on more than one occasion.

Giant Schnauzers are tough enough to take you down and keep you down. This one obviously has the right stuff. Note that the switch is being applied very lightly to develop invincibility in the dog. Photos courtesy of Alpha K-9 in Washington State.

After some time is spent targeting the sleeve and you are sure that the dog is going for the sleeve in a dependable fashion, you should start to run in a more natural fashion rather than with your arm way out to the side like a broken wing. Now you are going to keep it in a more natural position at your side and eventually you can even swing it back and forth just like the opposite arm. After he has advanced to this stage the proper presentation of the sleeve is with the elbow pointing rearward. The arm should be bent about 90 degrees, elbow rearmost. Held out from the body about 6 inches is just about right. This enables the dog's lower jaw some working room between the sleeve and your rib cage. Holding the sleeve tightly against your body is to invite a nip on the ribs or perhaps that shapely posterior that's made you famous. With your sleeve at the aforementioned angle, the hit should land on the meaty part (assuming you have a meaty part) of your forearm or elbow. If the arm is extended forward in a normal running mode, he may bite whatever is handy, or he may miss or slide off and go by you, doing a U-turn and coming again.

You may or may not be ready for it. If the arm is extended to the rear in the normal running mode, he may take your hand or wrist. Painful, especially if you're wearing the hidden sleeve. The answer is to run downfield without the arm swinging at all. It should ideally be stationary, elbow rearmost. If it swings in the

You can run, but you can't hide!

normal manner, it could be out of the dog's reach when he arrives. If it is, and you get a new scar, you've earned it. Make the sleeve a target. Remember, advanced dogs are taught to bite anywhere. If you give him the opportunity, he certainly will.

Approximately 95 percent of the time, Fido's angle of attack is roughly 45 degrees upward. Most of the time it will land him perfectly on your forearm given proper sleeve presentation. This information is offered in hopes of saving you some injuries. If you are silly enough to run downfield while looking straight ahead, you deserve whatever you get. In the interest of your own personal safety and/or survival, look behind you to see what the dog is doing. Why? Because he might be going to the wrong side. K-9 Nick

Norm Garner makes this Rottie work for the bite.

did this trick occasionally just to keep up his reputation and earn his nickname of "Sick Nick." More than a few South Florida K-9 handlers bear scars because they ran downfield looking straight ahead while Nick was closing the gap. It could have been worse. It could have been *Baby.*

The reason I'm spending so much time on this is because I saw many decoys injured unnecessarily while doing running apprehension work. Every single time the decoys were running downfield while looking straight ahead and swinging the sleeve in a natural manner. Our favorite decoy (Dennis) was never hurt catching Nick. A lot of other people were. Following my instructions, Dennis always looked over his shoulder.

All of the other decoys were looking straight ahead at the advice of their trainer. Injuries were the result and at least one

was injured more than once. You will learn different and sometimes conflicting methods of dog training. You decide which is best for you and again, let common sense and pain be your guide. My methods may not be the best or even the latest but they are definitely safer. The contents of this book come from experience, trial and error. It is my sincere hope that it will save you some valuable time and unnecessary injuries.

THE OUT

OK, now we've got the puppy biting like a Tyrannosaurus Rex. So, how do we get the little rascal off? Simple. We just say the word "out" and he immediately lets go and comes to a perfect heel at your side. If you believe that, I want to sell you some prime farm land as soon as the tide goes out. Seriously, any dog brought along in bite work in the fashion previously described will be quite spirited and biting very hard. Letting go will be the last thing on his mind. We will of course attempt to get him off with just a loud verbal command. Some dogs will out with just that, but it's a rare occurrence. When yours doesn't, don't get despondent. There are ways of getting the necessary response and I present them here for your edification.

1. THE STANDARD CHOKE chain is worn. When he doesn't out, a neck breaker of a snatch is done, making sure the choke is as high up on his neck as possible. On a determined dog, this is a light correction.

2. REPEAT #1 using a tight prong collar.

3. DUTCH OUT consider Fido's nose to be 12 o'clock, his tail six o'clock. Utilizing a chain or tie attached to his prong collar. The decoy approaches, takes the bite, then goes limp. Out command given followed by really hard snatches on the prong collar until he spits out the sleeve.

Once a good dog grabs hold, he won't let go. This bulldog is making good use of his natural "bite and hold" bullbaiting instincts.

out, secure him from six o'clock to something immovable. Secure him again from nine o'clock to an immovable object or a strong man with a 6-foot leash attached to his choke chain. Handler is at dog's three o'clock with a 6-foot leash

4. THE GAG the reed schlagstock or switch used in agitation can be used to out the dog pretty easily. The decoy takes the hit. While the dog is locked on, the decoy inserts the end of the switch into the dog's

Bite in deep water. The decoy, Mark Evans, is actually swimming with the dog attached. Talk about realistic training scenarios! This is very dangerous because the suit now weighs about 80 pounds soaking wet instead of a dry 25.

mouth between his upper jaw and his tongue. Being careful not to jab it down his throat he now puts pressure onto the back of the tongue with the stick. Presto! He's out. Works every time. Of course when the decoy is in position with the stick he nods to the handler who screams the out command into the dog's ear. The decoy does the jab immediately following the command. It works. The dog associates the gag with the handler's command. Two or three repeats are all that's necessary. Take care with the direction of the jab.

5. SHOCK COLLARS These little electric gizmos are the best thing since sliced bread and toilet paper. They not only provide an acceptable method of correction but they enable the handler to do it long-distance (which is the next best thing to being there). You see, they are radio controlled—no wires necessary. They've been around a long time now and as far as I'm concerned, they are perfected. The older ones zapped the dog as long as the button was held down. Newer models give only about a one-second jolt, then automatically shut off.

This prevents the heavy handed from torturing a dog into a gutless, neurotic bed-wetter. It has been done. I once got a very negative comment about shock collars from a respected trainer. He said he hated them because if you're using them in an electrical storm, they can go haywire and kill the dog.

However, I do have two criticisms of shock collars:

1. They are outrageously overpriced.

2. They are attached to a part of the dog that's practically insensitive to pain. Ever watch a bitch move her puppies? She invariably grabs the scruff of the neck and the puppy never makes a peep. It doesn't hurt. My theory is that there are very few pain sensors on a dog's neck. Any vet can tell you of the nearly total lack of a pain threshold on Bulldogs. Full-grown Bulldogs can be picked up by the scruff of their necks and held aloft until your arm gives out, and never make a sound. Point? Necks are tough, real tough.

The next point is that the dog's tough, insensitive neck becomes even more insensitive during the heat of battle. When in combat the adrenal glands go into red alert and the brain begins producing something called endorphins, which are the body's own little pain killers. If the dog is really hyped, it can be a real problem getting them off. When I purchased Nick, he weighed about 60 pounds and had the metabolism of a hummingbird. He lived for the bite. Though fully trained by another department, he was for sale because they couldn't make him out or recall. I figured if I couldn't change it, it was something I could live with. When I took Nick to training I noticed two things. He had to be strangled off every bite and the word "out" seemed to supercharge his efforts to hold the bite. I thought that since he had never made the connection with that word, I should substitute another word for it that he had already made the connection with. The word was *leave.* It would make him stop urinating in midstream, stop drinking water, or stop playing with his ball. He knew what it meant and that he should obey it.

Building prey drive on a Doberman.

Quick Dobie ("Sassy") trying to get under the sleeve.

My next dilemma was to provide a new incentive to heed the command. The former trainer told me everything in the world had been tried, including prong collars, shock collars, the works. In fact, he said the old-fashioned shock collar (the type that continues shocking as long as the button is depressed) only revved him up. This dog's fighting drive, adrenaline and endorphin level apparently went right off the scale. I needed something diabolically effective. Years ago my vet had told me about a gland at the base of the tail that produces oil for the coat. In the area of this gland were lots of capillaries and pain sensors. Fleas love this area because of the easy access to the capillaries near the surface of

the skin. Due to the many pain sensors there, the dog really reacts to the flea bite and either licks or chews the area that stimulates the gland. So, even though they cause him discomfort, the fleas provide a service by making Fido lick the area which results in a shiny coat. By now you're wondering what my point may be. It is simply that I found the chink in the armor that I hoped would have this crazy dog outing cleanly. I don't own a shock collar and couldn't think of a way to attach it to the dog's butt if I did. I do, however, own a flashlight known as...

6. "THE SOURCE" At the rear end of the light is an electric stinger very similar to the shock collar. It was a kind of a forerunner to the "stun gun." I put Nick on the sleeved decoy. Next I grabbed his tail at its base and applied the device exactly 1 inch in front of the tail. I bellowed the command *"Leave!"* and zapped him. He spit out the sleeve like it was on fire and turned to see what had bit him. As far as he knew, it was me because "The Source" was already back in my pocket. We repeated the exercise one more time. Nick never required a refresher. He outed cleanly for the rest of his life. His former name had been Major and he had been nicknamed "Crazy Maj" by all who knew him. I hated the name and the nickname and changed it to Nick so as not to scare my already nervous chief. Within one week

A tight prong collar is an effective tool for tough dogs who are not so apt to out on command.

the guys I trained with dubbed him "Sick Nick" and it stuck. He became famous in K-9 circles. If they didn't know his name, they just referred to him as "That crazy dog." He had more heart and more drive than could be measured, but he outed cleanly.

7. THE NERVE This method is really tough on the dog and should be saved for last because, frankly, it's cruel. It works, but it causes the dog a lot of pain no matter how hyped he is. It is so severe that I caution you not to mess with it unless under the supervision of a master trainer. In the hands of an amateur it could ruin the dog forever by teaching him to run from a stick. Assuming the decoy is right handed and catching with his left, strike the dog's upper left leg about two-and-one-half inches below the elbow. Strike hard and continue to strike until he outs. He absolutely WILL out, but you will feel bad about it because he will scream like nothing you can imagine. Exercise extreme care not to hit the elbow, because you can break it even though you're using only the light reed schlagstock. It goes without saying that you strike immediately after the out command. The dog must see this pain as following the handler's command to release. If the previous six techniques have failed, you better believe he's a hard dog. This one won't fail, although I can't overstress the importance of using this technique last.

8. THE BACK DOOR The following technique I have actually never tried but have heard of many times, mostly from owners of catch dogs which are invariably bulldogs of one sort or another. I say if it can get an angry bulldog off a wild boar, it should work on anything. It is as follows: either a smooth hardwood stick or real attention getter. Try it on your dog and let me know how it works. Just don't confuse the sequence of events. Licking your finger is the *first* thing you do! Good luck.

9. THE DECOY OUT A Your decoy can teach Fido the out. Fido wears a prong collar with a short leash hanging underneath. When he bites,

Bandit shook the author so hard on this hit that his right arm was badly bruised from the sleeve slamming back and forth. He was the most awesome dog Mike Harlow ever had on his arm.

finger is first lubricated by wetting it with saliva. The opposite hand grabs the base of the tail tightly. The now lubricated "device" is poked quickly into the tight little orifice you will find directly under the tail. I am told it is a the decoy reaches under the sleeve and gets hold of the short leash. The handler shouts the command word to release and the decoy gives the correction towards himself from under the sleeve. Works great.

10. THE DECOY OUT B A very similar technique with less trauma. Instead of a prong collar the decoy is armed with a spritzer bottle that he keeps concealed behind the sleeve. When handler shouts release command, the decoy sprays Fido in the face with water. It works.

11. THE HARLOW OUT I've saved the best for last. It is so effective that it makes every method preceding it obsolete in my opinion. Let's say you are starting a tough dog that lacked the advantage of being trained to out on toys as a puppy. Since the start of this book I've had the opportunity to train ten different American Bulldogs, three Rottweilers and four Dobermans. Just like the puppies, these dogs were grabbed by the ears (by their handlers). The handlers were then instructed to scream the release command into the face of their dog with enough volume to blow the whiskers off their faces. In every single case, the dogs outed immediately and were praised accordingly. I'm still waiting for the first failure.

So far, the only mishap occurred when Mark Locey utilized this method with his American Bulldog, Sonny. Sonny was so startled by Mark's loud command that he released and jerked his head back. Unfortunately, Mark was standing behind him and caught the top of Sonny's head square in the face. Seeing that Mark was hurt and his eyes were filled with yellow menace,

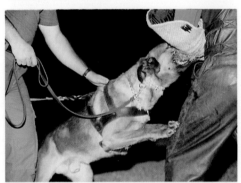

Static line agitation using a non-restrictive harness. Bob Anderson demonstrating the "gag" release on a Belgian Malinois. Handler is praising his dog for this intense performance.

I reminded him to praise his dog for the beautiful out. His eyes now watering from the pain, Mark got down and hugged Sonny's neck saying "good boy" through clenched teeth. Sonny had outed cleanly ever since without a single correction. So have the other 16

dogs exposed to this technique.

Bill Koehler's method of non-communicative obedience training, combined with the progressive recall and the "Harlow" method of outing the dog will save you countless hours of training and frustration and failure. There are no intelligent reasons for deviating from this formula.

THE SAFETY FACTOR

After my dog is trained to bite, will it be safe to have him around people who are innocent, law-abiding citizens? This may sound like a stupid question to a canine handler or a Schutzhund person, but remember how much you knew about canine behavior before you attained your current Ph.D. on the subject? ZIP! So for the new guys to this fascinating vocation, let me open your eyes (and the eyes of the insurance industry) on the comparative levels of safety between the trained dog versus the untrained dog. Of course we will assume that we are talking about identical breeds who are of the proper temperament to do protection work. A dog with good guard potential is going to have a certain potential for biting people. People who are not known to the dog will have a higher risk than family members and close friends of the family.

Bad guy being searched while dog watches closely. Passive stranger gets ugly. K-9 reacts accordingly. Getting down with dog teaches him he can win. Bob earns his money.

The dog doesn't fear humans and he should have instincts that will make him defend his family and property. The difficulty arises in his perception of an evildoer as compared to yours and the law's perception of evildoer—there may be a wide gap. I heard it said by people who told me they were smarter than me that a mature dog has the intelligence of a five-year-old child. My experience tells me this is a pretty accurate guess. I generally don't trust the judgment of a five-year-old child, but I've found out they can be taught some very helpful things if it is kept simple. At this age, your child can and should know his address and phone number and his parents' names. Dogs trained as outlined in this text will know the difference between good and bad people simply by the programming done in beginning agitation. Passive walk-bys by the agitator are the foundation of his learning process, and teach him he can't bite the guy unless an overly aggressive move is made toward him or his master (or later on, the property). When the passive walk-by is done by the decoy, you discourage him from biting the guy. When the passive walk-by turns aggressive, he is encouraged to react with a bite. He is praised when he does.

This will with repetition create a dog who will let a passive stranger walk by, but he will be closely watched. The passive stranger that *occasionally* slaps the dog when his guard is down

Future man-stoppers? Some of those great Blackwell AB pups. Preacher on far right.

trains Sparky to maintain the eternal vigilance that we hear so much about and see so little of. If the passive decoy is allowed to slap the dog every time or even every other time, you will create a dog who is too quick on the trigger. It will vary with the dog, but a sneaky slap two times out of ten is usually all that's necessary to arouse your dog's dormant distrust of the stranger. He is *always* scolded for making a try for a passive walk-by. Your dog has a good memory and in short order he will know who he can bite and who he can't. The untrained dog may or may not. The untrained dog may or may not "out" on command. The trained dog *will*. This will be true of both police dogs *and* home guardians. In case the foregoing was too wordy, I'll break it down so that there is no possible confusion.

The trained dog is more controllable and because of this, he is less dangerous and less of a liability. If your insurance company is charging you a higher premium because you keep a trained dog, I suggest you drop them like a hot rock. They are bottom feeders. The only thing worse is being dropped by the company as my police dog was after three years service and a perfect record of no bad bites and not a single lawsuit. There were times when having Nick meant the difference between leaving bodies in the street and to coast several times. Insurance companies should offer discounts to police agencies who use trained dogs. Dropping them is an obscenity. Nick saved them millions. Nick was not alone. Every police dog in Florida was also dropped. The departments not big enough to self-insure got out of the K-9 business.

Over the jump and into the bite. Exercises like this have twofold purpose: one, to develop the dog's leg and hip muscles and two, to develop skills necessary for real-world pursuit situations.

simply clearing the street during a riot. We were even borrowed by other departments to help with riots outside our jurisdiction. The riots were defused because we had the dogs. Without the dogs, I'm sure we would have made the six o'clock news coast

Not every company dropped the dogs. A few agreed to insure dogs that could pass state guidelines of minimum standards of control. There is still no state-mandated certification of police dogs in the state of Florida. They have had the proposed standards for years. Don't ask me what the holdup is; I can't imagine.

To get back to the original subject of safety, the other part of your training that ensures a safe, well-rounded dog is to have the decoy drop the training sleeve, walk up and pet the dog after the agitation and eventually have him walking up to the dog with it on. The dog shouldn't key on the sleeve, but on the aggressive behavior of the decoy. If spectators appear while training, allow them to pet the dogs afterward. Constant socialization reinforces the dog's dual personality (tough dog/ sweet dog). A typical example is my son Brent sitting on Rock right after he was shaking my fillings loose on the training sleeve. Rock isn't even my dog. It is typical Bulldog behavior. I do not recommend that with other breeds as a regular practice. Patch and Rock are the first Pit Bull and American Bulldog I've trained for protection and I'm amazed at the instant switch back to the sweet-dog mode and the controllability. These two breeds really want to please. I can't recommend them strongly enough. If you are in doubt about the credibility of my recommendation, get one and try it. I think even the most dyed-in-the-wool German Shepherd lover will admire these breeds if they will try one. Personality, brains, ability, heart and astonishing strength are the hallmarks of these two breeds.

One other reason to train your guard dog: when your dog is trained he is made to believe that no man can be any serious threat to him. He has learned that he wins every fight he gets into during his training period. Knowing that he is the toughest S.O.B. in the valley, he will fear no evil and as a direct result of this, he becomes a very calm fellow. He develops a new attitude that all is well with the world because he has deemed it so. Having been around lots of them I can assure you that the safest dogs I've ever been around are experienced police dogs. Not only are they more placid but they even seem to develop more interesting personalities as a direct result of not worrying about a new stranger. They already know they can kick your butt; the need to prove it is no longer prevalent for them. It's kind of like being six-feet eight-inches tall and being 270 pounds of rippling muscle. You are not in fear of imminent attack.

It is therefore my qualified opinion that the best thing you could possibly do for your rough, tough guard dog is to put him through a training curriculum similar to the one outlined in this text. The pride of ownership that you will derive will outweigh the time and expense that you invested. Do it.

It was my plan to teach my current dog the "out" before progressing to bitework. Due to all the rumors flying around about the near-impossibility of getting the various "Bull" breeds

Red nose APBT Giants Diesel, a superior athlete. This dog hits a sleeve so hard that he injures shoulders and hips. He is a stud dog for Land of Giants APBT kennel in Athol, Massachusetts.

to out on command, I saw this as an opportunity to test two things:

1. If indeed the rumors are true about Bulldogs being nearly impossible to out. After all, they were bred for their tenacity.

2. Just how good, if at all, is the technique of teaching the out before the bite.

As a fair test of the rumor of Bulldogs being out-proof, I thought it wouldn't be completely fair unless both of the breeds that I tout as being the top breeds for protection and police work were tested side by side. Since I already owned an American Bulldog, I only needed an American Pit Bull Terrier. No sweat—they are common in the West Palm Beach area that I call home. A quick call to my friend Lance Jackson got me the Pit Bull and a willing decoy for my

dog. Both dogs were obedience-trained. Both dogs definitely knew who their bosses were and both dogs passed tests that satisfied me that they had the right stuff. Lance's dog wasn't trained formally in O.B but he was very well behaved and never challenged Lance. He is a male and moderately huge for a Pit Bull. Rock goes about 90 lbs. My dog is moderately sized female American Bulldog going about 70 lbs.

Contrary to the current plague of yellow journalism circulating about Pit Bulls being instruments of Satan, Rock is a *typical* example of the breed. That is, a totally trustworthy, super-social, tail-wagging sweety pie. He may look like 90 lbs. of white death, but he's really quite willing to let just about anyone in the world walk up to him and pet him. He's a pushover for a scratch behind the ear.

My dog is not the sweety pie Rock is. She is more skeptical and untrusting of strangers. She has an escalating level of distrust that is geared to the size of the individual. She views kids as no threat whatsoever and lets them not only approach but allows them to immediately maul her. Most women are permitted a brief scratch on the head for openers and are discouraged from further advances until she knows them better. Very few grown men are allowed to approach. The larger the man, the more serious the warning. After about 30 minutes almost anybody becomes family. This canine skepticism is common among good guard breeds and is practically extinct among some of the family-type tail-waggers like Labs, Golden Retrievers, etc.

For the uninitiated, this should not be confused with shyness or being vicious or fearful, just the opposite—she fears nothing. Her survival instincts are alive and well as opposed to the Lab, who is actually naive to possible threats in his environment. His survival instincts are so repressed that they may as well be non-existent. This is what makes them good mascots for the firehouse or the ski lodge, but lousy watchdogs. Labs tend to love everybody. American Bulldogs tend to love family and familiar friend—not strangers. This canine skepticism is commonly referred to as

"hardness" by professional trainers. It is what they look for in prospective Schutzhund candidates, a good indicator that the dog in question will do protection work.

Both dogs were staked out on heavy cable and chain respectively. Rock was first up. At my approach, he was totally relaxed. He quietly watched in curious fascination as I got

Civil agitation. Lots of verbal abuse, taunting and running as in a riot. Preacher and Patch. ABs really test equipment.

sneaky and started making my movements quick and furtive. To my curious fascination, he would not bark; he was *too* relaxed! When I finally screamed and rushed him, he torpedoed me and got a nice bite first time out but never made a sound. I gave him a brief easy fight with the sleeve, then dropped it and limped away screaming.

The bite was not a bone crusher, but it was solid and completely acceptable for the first bite. He was allowed to play with the sleeve as a reward and of course got lots of praise from

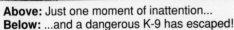

Above: Just one moment of inattention...
Below: ...and a dangerous K-9 has escaped!

his master. Patch was up next. She didn't need any agitation other than a hard stare. She lit up like a Christmas tree, slinging snot and doing backflips. When she realized that Lance wasn't coming close enough to donate blood, she finally settled for the sleeve. Not a great bite, but a bite nonetheless. She was allowed to have the sleeve as a trophy also, but lost interest quickly when she realized Lance wasn't in it.

Rock's second time at bat was much better. I came in closer and he got a very deep, full-mouth bite and shook me a bit. I slipped the sleeve and ran off screaming. That got a serious tail wag out of him. Rock's third time up we fought briefly; I went limp and Lance tried a verbal out. He complied immediately. He received lots of praise and a hug. He has outed cleanly every time since. Patch's second time up resulted in a much-improved bite for the same reason as Rock's second bite. I came in closer; Lance came in closer. She got a deep full-mouth bite. When Lance went limp, I got down low and put my face against hers and barked "out" like a Marine drill sergeant. She spit the sleeve like it was on fire. I praised her highly and gave her a big hug. We repeated this exercise many times. Both dogs are now outing cleanly every time without fail.

I'm tempted to charge extra for revealing the following training secret on why these out of control, vicious, monster

Rode Hawg kennels' American Bulldog Bandit.

Bulldogs are acting in a manner that conflicts directly with everything previously printed about them (particularly the Pit Bull).

Phase two of the test proves rather emphatically that teaching the out before the bite not only works quickly but works without a single correction, resulting in no confusion for the dogs, no trauma, no mental anguish, no pouting and no setbacks.

Now for the mere purchase price of this book you are going to learn the grizzly, dark secret of how we tortured these hapless creatures into releasing their deadly grip on a verbal command. I hope the reader has a strong stomach. Here goes:

Patch was taken out into a large grassy field way out in the country away from the prying eyes of humaniacs and the news media. She was off-lead at a heel when I made my insidious first move. I threw an 8-inch red rubber ring out into the grass and yelled "Fetch" as she broke into a run after the irresistible rolling toy. Having a strong prey drive, Bulldogs are natural retrievers. In order to get her to bring it to me after the fetch, I yell the word "Bring" and start to run away from her if she doesn't come right away. She can't resist *any* chance to beat me in a footrace, so here she comes! When she gets near, I drop onto my knees with arms outspread, which has already been programmed into her head to mean come and get a hug, something else she can't resist. When she gets there I don't disappoint her—she gets the hug. While she's getting her hug and lots of verbal praise, I'm getting my hand on the ring. I now take a deep breath and firm grip on the ring and pull it toward me as I bend over. I actually place my face against hers and bark the word "out" like a drill sergeant. Very guttural. Because she has already learned who the boss is, she doesn't question my command. She is aware that I am the alpha dog in her pack and immediately relinquishes the ring. I immediately praise the hell out of her and give her another brief hug. Three or four repeats per day for three or four days and it is indelibly programmed into her brain that "out" means release and I fortify each lesson with praise. Pretty hair raising? You bet. It's why they pay me the big bucks.

Rock was taught to release the bite in exactly the same manner by his master, who never *met* a trainer. I say this because I learned the idea from a trainer during a long-distance phone call. He told me only after swearing me to secrecy because he learned it from a well-known hotshot trainer from Europe who still guards his training secrets like the Holy Grail. The trainer I talked to wouldn't tell me the details of the technique, only the basic concept. Lance taught Rock the same release trick by

accident, never suspecting he would one day be protection-training the beast (and finding the early toy training to prove so valuable).

I don't know if this will work on every tough dog in the world, but it worked on not one, but *two* of those stoneheaded Bulldogs. One of the two things has to be a fact: either Bulldogs are easy to train because of their willingness to please, or I am an absolute magician when it comes to the training of dogs. You decide.

Just as an aside, Patch is being trained to recall in exactly the same manner—with the red rubber ring. When she gets her first chance to recall from a running man, I can virtually guarantee she will do it the first time and every time and never need a correction. I can't guarantee success for you because I have no way of knowing if you are following the instructions to the letter. You might also be handicapping yourself by using a German Shepherd or something. Who knows? Anyway, I strongly urge you to try these techniques *first*. They might save you a great deal of your valuable time in producing a finished dog. I'm probably not going to scrap the

Opposite: The following series of photos is from Patch's first time on the bitesuit, on day ten of bitework. She got in some good bites and refused to be slung off, despite the decoy's efforts. That's the author in the upper right-hand photo giving lots of verbal encouragement and praise. The headlock in the last photo only increased her drive.

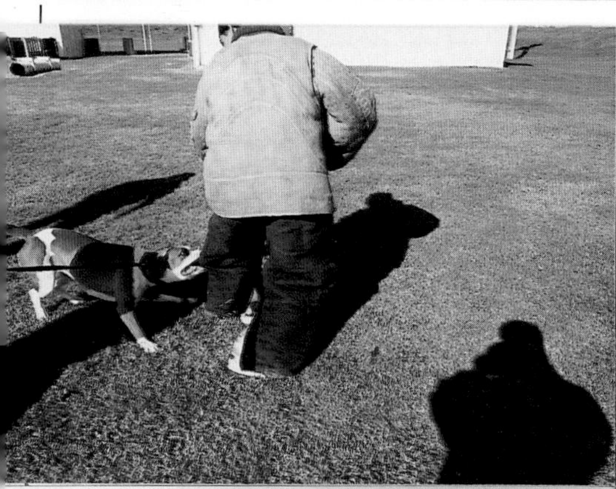

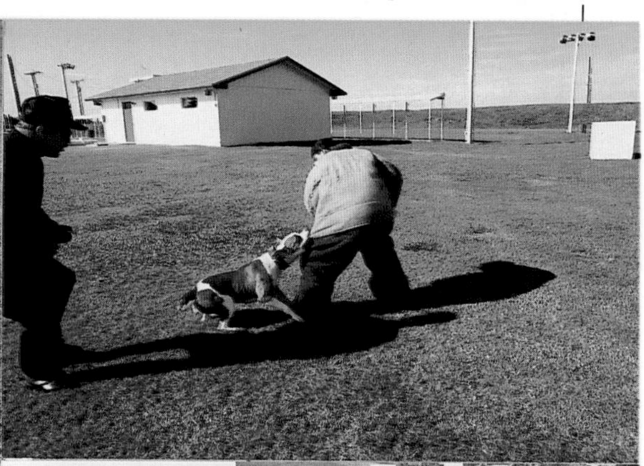

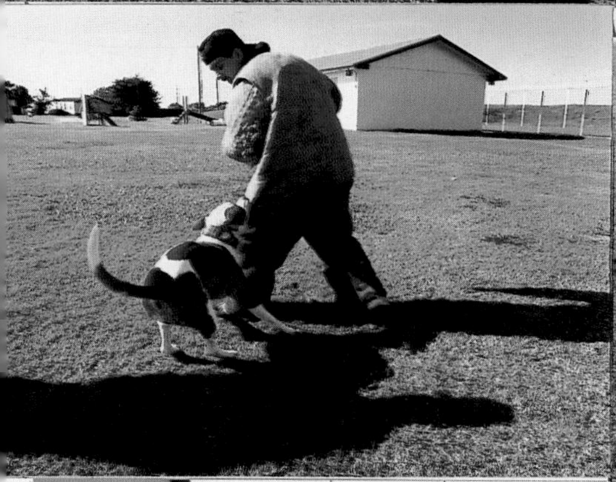

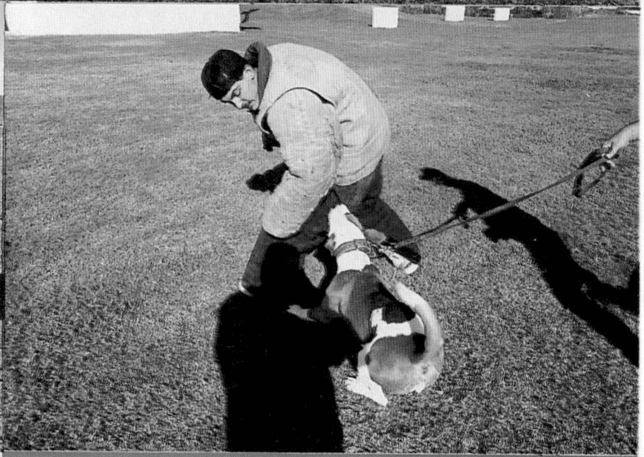

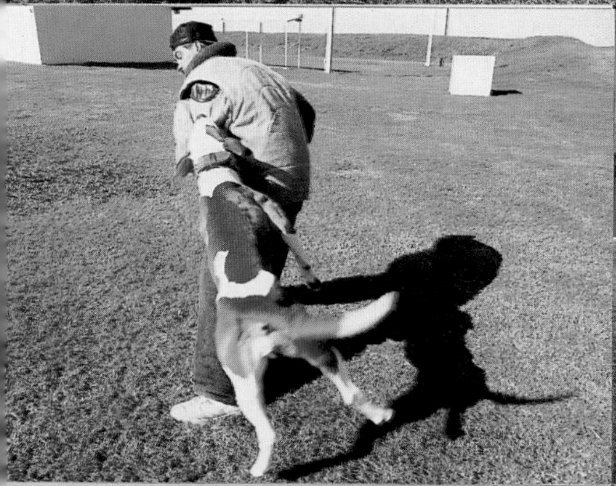

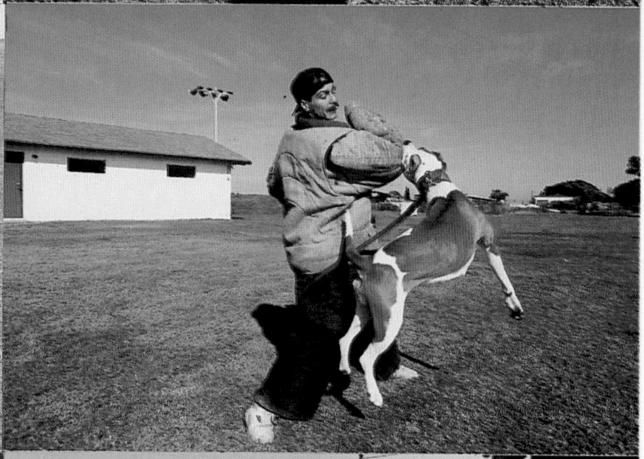

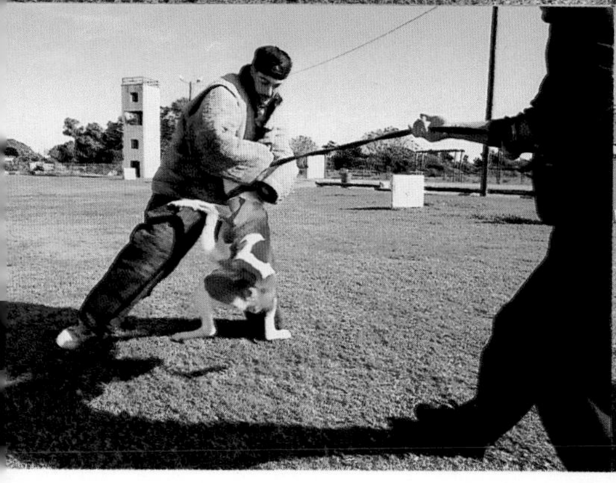

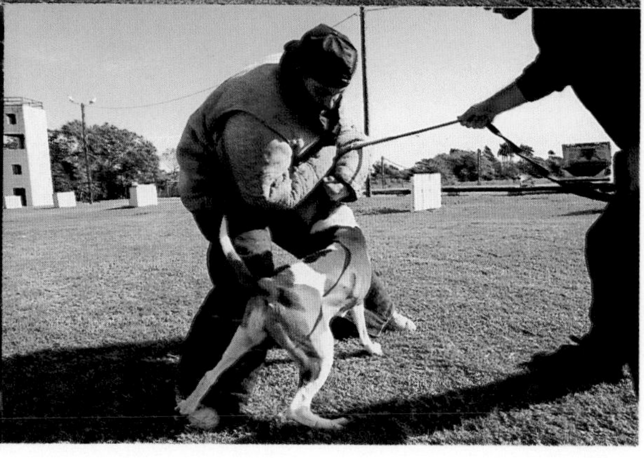

other techniques I've listed for getting the beast to "out" and "recall," but they will be used only after these two techniques fail. You see, the most enjoyable part of dog training is when you can show off a finished dog. Utilizing these two methods can make it happen a lot quicker.

DEBUNKING YET ANOTHER MYTH

One of the things I've heard over the years from German Shepherd owners especially is that Bulldogs can't track. This recurring bit of ignorance usually rears its ugly head every time someone starts fantasizing about one of the Bulldog breeds being used as a police dog (me mostly). I remember hearing the same crap when the Rottweiler was still rare in police work. This myth has always been a major source of irritation for me, but never so much as when I hear it from breeders of Pit Bulls and, to a lesser extent, from American Bulldog breeders. Some of these people actually hunt hogs with their dogs with great success. The usual formula is several trail dogs and one "catch dog." The theory being that the trail dogs will bay the hog and nip at it while waiting for the Bulldog to arrive and sort out the hog. Once the

The author and K-9 Nero, one tough Belgian Malinois owned by Sgt. Ron Shunk. In the top photo, Nero gets a good armpit bite—this was supposed to be of a high chest bite, but Nero lost his nerve at the last second. The last two photos are running apprehension. As you can see, Nero put him down hard.

bay dogs see that Old Crusher's got a good ear hold, the bay dogs come in and lend a hand. The owner of the catch dog has no problem discerning that his bay dogs are smart enough to let the specialist (catch dog) do what he does best, but they seem to have a real problem giving Bulldogs credit for being smart enough (when they're running with the pack) to let the trailing specialists (trail dogs) do what they're best at: tracking.

It is always thought by most dog men that the catch dogs must be stupid for going right for the head of a wild boar. I have reminded them on many occasions that that's where the weapons are and that is what needs to be immobilized. Bulldogs are smart enough to know that it's the only way anyone's going to bring home the bacon. They're also the only one in this intrepid group of hunters with the stones to just wade in there and do it. Everyone else (to include the brave dog owner) waits for the Bulldog to make his all-important "first move." While the Bulldog is holding the hog's head, no one else is getting sliced up. Dumb? I think not. Going for the hind quarters is dumb; it can get a dog killed. Even the biggest hogs in the woods can swap ends faster then you can say, "Don't do it." Bulldogs almost always go straight for the head.

A lot of hog hunters think that just because Bulldogs will let the traildogs do the work of tracking, that the Bulldogs can't

track. This belief is because these same hog hunters have never tried it from the night-poaching perspective. Don't get excited, neither have I, but I knew a man who did it on a regular basis and his method was as follows: because his act was illegal, he needed the cover of darkness and he needed to do it quietly because of the close proximity of the land owner's home. The only way to hunt hog quietly is with a dog that doesn't bay. Quite naturally, bay dogs were out. Catch dogs can't be hunted together because of the possibility of fights. So how did he do it? You guessed it—with one Pit Bull and a pocket knife. When alone, his Pit Bull simply did her own tracking and she did it quietly and did it well. When she ran in the pack, she let the experts do the tracking.

Lest you skeptics think that I'm relying on hearsay from a criminal, I have also been tracking with my American Bulldog and Lance's Pit Bull. Rock was reluctant at first to put his nose on the ground, but when I was finally able to talk him into it, he followed the track just like any other dog and found his master hiding in bushes. Patch needed no coaxing at all when it came time for her to find me. She put her nose down where Lance pointed and they were off. She never lifted her nose until she found me.

So the next time someone tells you that Bulldogs can't track, you will know that they have never tried a Bulldog or that they don't know to teach a dog tracking.

RECALL—THE ULTIMATE CHALLENGE

This is of course the strongest argument in favor of the trained dog versus the use of deadly force. The dog is not considered deadly force for the obvious reason that he is not trained to kill. Yes, sending him can be a mistake just as firing a bullet can. The bullet, however, can't be called back once it is launched. I once worked a dog that never recalled either in training or in competition— never. On the street in real situations, though, he recalled seven out of seven times. Experienced trainers love telling me that in real situations there is a pronounced urgency in my voice that isn't present in training. The difference of reality versus training is the obvious sleeve. Even the so-called "hidden" sleeve is conspicuously larger in diameter than the bare arm. Now older and smarter, I have come to realize that my dog never knew that I wanted him to stop chasing the bad guy and return to me. He was a smart dog and perfectly willing to please if you just showed him how. That's the secret. It was so simple that it was difficult. The key to teaching "Sick Nick" the recall was hiding in plain sight. We tried everything we could think of to get Nick to recall and everything failed. So was Nick a hopeless bonehead? Not at all,

we just couldn't get his attention. Whenever practicing running apprehensions, the dog developed a singleness of purpose that was scary. He literally developed tunnel vision and went deaf to all outside activity or communications. This is a very real phenomenon in human psychology known as tachapsychia. In certain situations where adrenaline is in abundant supply, such as car wrecks and fights (especially gunfights), people develop these symptoms even to the point of not hearing gunshots and seeing movement in slow motion. Some cops even report seeing the bullets coming out of the bad guy's gun! Well, I can't say if Nick saw things in slow motion, but I can guarantee that he went deaf and locked into tunnel vision, focusing solely on the running decoy with the abnormally large arm. Don't believe it? Read on.

When I say we tried everything on him, I mean it!: verbal commands, the standard choke, prong collars, electric collars, physical force...and worse. His initial training was at the Lee Co. Sheriff's Office in the capable hands of Sgt. Steve Lux, their trainer at that time.

Just before his retirement I heard of something called the standing recall where the decoy ran out, stopped when he heard the dog get recalled and would stand passively with arms at his sides. I got my favorite decoy, Dennis Hodges, and we began. Nick still went all the way to the

Sure Grips Hog Dog. The leather armor protects him from the tusks of the wild boar he catches.

decoy but the bite was half-hearted. The second time was only a nip! We were on the edge of a breakthrough. A couple times out of 20 Nick actually stopped short and barked. When I ran down to him he would come back with me but he sure didn't like it. All the way back he would watch Dennis over his shoulder in hopes of seeing the slightest provocation. So what's the point? Nick was the victim of programmed response and tachapsychia (tunnel vision). The programmed response was the routine of our running apprehension work. We always did it the same—a guy with a fat arm running away. With tachapsychia comes partial or

total deafness. He definitely wasn't hearing me. He couldn't *see* my disappointment for two reasons: Tunnel vision doesn't allow it and I was behind him. When Nick was brought to the starting line for a catch, he was so bite-motivated that his brain automatically clicked into tachapsychia mode. It was scary to watch. His yellow eyes would go to pinpoints and I could literally punch him in the head without him noticing. His eyes would not blink and would not leave the decoy, or more accurately the sleeve. On a false start one night (decoy runs, dog breaks without command), I broke a heavy leather leash trying to snatch him back to the

J.D. Blackwell's Spice and Buster Brown as puppies.

heel. He weighed 70 pounds. The leash came back with such force that it left a painful welt on my abdomen.

Lest I stray too far from the standing recall: what's different about it? Simple. The man stops and goes passive. That was not part of Nick's programming. It threw him into such a state of confusion that it broke the steel grip of the tachapsychia long enough for him to hear his furious handler screaming *"NO!"* Unfortunately that one single session was the only session we were ever able to attempt. Our insurance ran out and the company refused to carry police dogs anymore because the dogs were perceived as a potential liability. We had never been sued or even had a complaint lodged against us. The insurance company had never even seen Nick. As the bony fingers of the insurance industry are pried from the framework of ignorance on which they are based, this policy *will* change. When that

day comes, insurance companies will refuse to insure police agencies who *don't* have dogs.

I'm sure we were on the right track with the standing recall. I'm certain we were about to have "Sick Nick" recalling just like he was a normal dog.

Just to illustrate how I am still learning dog training techniques, I will share one more that I think borders on brilliance. The traditional method of teaching recall to your dog is to be standing next to him when the decoy starts downfield at a run. You count about three seconds then send the dog. You then scream the recall command from *behind* your dog who may very well be in a state of tachapsychia. Behind him might be the worst place to be if he is in tachapsychia. Since he won't hear you or see you, can you guess where you're going to stand? Right. Somewhere between the decoy and your dog. Why? So that your tunnel-visioned little pal can see you, that's why. Is this brilliant or what? It was so simple, it evaded me for years. In search for the complex solution, I walked right past a simple one. Jumping into the tunnel had simply never occurred to me. Since long, hard-to-pronounce psychological words don't make much of an impression on the old memory and since the shrinks will blanch at the thought of my applying such a term to a non-human, I hereby dub K-9 tachapsychia as "Sick Nick Syndrome," or S.N.S. for short. I was so impressed with the results of this technique that I asked the name of it. Sgt. Bobby Anderson coined the name "progressive recall."

Progressive recall means the handler stands roughly halfway between his dog and the decoy. When the dog goes, he literally jumps in front of him to break his concentration, or if

dog. By that time, Fido has made the connection and knows what you want. He learned what you wanted in spite of his tunnel vision because you jumped into the tunnel and yelled the halt command.

Does this method work? Like nothing else I've ever seen. Judging from what I saw, when it's properly done it works

Fujima Max at 16 months, 90 pounds. From Rode Hawg kennels.

applicable S.N.S., by throwing him into a state of confusion (remember, this deviates from his normal routine), short-circuiting his normal "programmed response." He puts on the brakes. Quite naturally the handler praises him to the maximum. The distance between dog and handler gradually or progressively diminishes to the point where the handler is at the dog's side when he sends the

virtually 100 percent of the time. Where I come from, that's a passing score. Lest I forget, the dog is on a long line and prong collar, but the only time it was necessary was when a rookie handler forgot to flag down his dog and stood silent as the dog hurtled past in pursuit of the decoy. I am really impressed with the technique. It works. As far as I'm concerned all other techniques are primitive in comparison and I watched them all fail miserably on Nick. The standing recall will in all probability work but why waste valuable time waiting for it to take hold? There are two other little tricks that will reinforce the recall and that are deserving of mention. One is called backbiting. When the recall is given, a second decoy attacks the handler, giving Fido a good reason to return to his handler. The second one is done by the handler tossing Fido's toy to the sideline for him to fetch, but I suspect it will only work on a ball freak. Both tricks are dependent on your dog looking at you, and trying to decide if he's coming back. If he's caught in the steely grip of S.N.S., it won't work.

I'm told the Dutch police are having success with a variation of this progressive recall. They use a stranger to jump up and chase the dog back to the handler. So try it already.

With the introduction of the progressive recall, it is no longer necessary for anyone to have a dog that won't recall. I'm sure the ultimate test would have been to try it with Nick, but because the standing recall was right on the hair edge of success, I'm positive that the progressive method would have worked even on him. He was, after all, a controllable, intelligent and affectionate dog. He was no psycho and I'm sure that all the guys wearing scars from him have forgiven him, just as I have forgiven Doug Madigan's "Baby."

MORE RANDOM THOUGHTS

During my tenure as a police K-9 handler, I became aware of an organization known as the United States Police Canine Association. It is a club whose purpose is to promote the training and use of dogs in police work; to stimulate new ideas in this area by the sanctioning of competitions throughout the country; and to provide a very necessary security blanket for the man/dog teams by awarding certifications that affirm that man and his dog have demonstrated a level of knowledge, skill and control that meets or exceeds the association's requirements. This certification carries with it a degree of prestige in that they don't give it away, but more importantly it carries weight that can come in handy in court if the officer is being sued. It makes it difficult for plaintiff's council to discredit the quality of your dog's training. Since there is no national (and in most cases no state) guidelines as to what makes an acceptable police dog, it is wise to join an organization of this type and endeavor to attain certification from them.

There is, however, a fly in the ointment. You see, the key word here is competition. Attaining the minimum points needed will win certification, but big beautiful trophies, plaques, medals, ribbons, etc., are awarded to those attaining yet more points. Everything sounds OK so far, right? Well, over the years the training has improved

K-9 Nero standing on top of the world.

so much that nearly everyone could be winning or tying for the top prizes, so naturally the requirements had to become more and more demanding. The requirements are now competition-oriented. It is my opinion and the opinion of many trainers that these dog trials are geared to competition dogs rather than street dogs (real police dogs). The trainers and I agree that having the dogs ready for the street and having them ready for competition are two entirely different things. What a shame. The dogs learn how to work the street, then two to six weeks before competition they start working on the competition drill. I think this is hard on them. They are only dogs, after all. My criticism of the Schutzhund bark and hold routine can be repeated for USPCA competition events. They do something similar.

Following an apprehension, the dog is called off to a sit/stay and guard while the handler searches the suspect for weapons. Every law-enforcement agency I'm aware of teaches officers to cuff first, then search. Why should it be different in USPCA competition? Every K-9 unit I'm acquainted with leaves the dog on the suspect until he is cuffed. Then the dog is outed and the search commences. This is how it's done on the street to ensure officer safety. Either the USPCA is unaware of this officer safety technique or they just don't care about it; I'm not sure which. Their intent in this exercise is to measure the dog's controllability in a stress situation. That's good, but not at the expense of officer safety.

In Holland, there is a type of police-dog training that has a lot going for it: KNPV. KNPV is geared toward reality and perhaps the USPCA should take a close look at it. The Dutch aren't so all-fired concerned about a perfect heel. They are concerned with how well he does real police work. One novel idea that I'd like to see is professional decoys. They run out of sight

Banuelos Predator SchH II WH, the first Schutzhund-titled American Bulldog in history.

and hide. The dog is sent in to retrieve him. It's done completely out of sight of the judge. When the decoy is dragged out to the handler and judge, the decoy tells the judge yes or no. I like that. You have no business judging a dog's bite unless he is biting *you*.

Another criticism of USPCA is of their box search event. A man hides in one of six boxes after stinking up all the boxes. The dog must find the box with the most scent (hot box), and give a discernible indication that the man is inside the box (barking, scratch, whining or digging). At our last competition my dog got the right box and did it more quickly than all the others. Did he win a prize? No, he was instead penalized for searching too fast! I explained to the judge that he always searched fast and that he was never wrong. It was just this particular dog's style. Too bad, next dog!

Nick never did miss a box, by the way. Never. If he said they were there, they were there. He never lost a man on the street either. He once tracked a man for a quarter mile to a difficult barbed-wire fence. To negotiate the fence I would have had to drop the leash and he was so wired on this track, I was afraid to do it; track aborted. Ten minutes later the suspect was spotted downtown with pants that were wet to the knees. After tracking him in knee-high grass, so were mine. We put him against a wall with three other creatures of the night who were too nosy to keep walking when they saw the patrol cars. I walked Nick past all four on lead and said "check." He stopped at the guy with the wet pants and fired up. I arrested him. Ten minutes later at the police station, he confessed and said, "That's one hell of a dog." I couldn't have agreed more. I don't think I would have tried to use Nick as my sole reason for arrest, though it gave me reasonable grounds to question him. His confession corroborated my suspicions and it certainly lifted my spirits after seeing Nick penalized earlier in the day for searching too fast, of all things.

Am I telling anyone not to join USPCA? Not at all, but maybe some of the influential members will read this and change some of the rules so as to comply with what happens on the street. I believe the main goal of the USPCA should be the creation of that security blanket of certification of qualified police dogs. I think they have lost sight of this goal and have instead gone astray, making circus dogs instead of police dogs.

The North American Working Dog Association uses a pass/fail system of judging the dogs. That sounds good to me although I have no knowledge of their criteria. If they are geared more to *real* dogs, I applaud them. The interview I read in USPCA's *Canine Courier* magazine indicated that they are. Any dog handlers who have been unable to meet the elitist standards of the one may find a warm spot by the fire at the other. It would behoove you to join at least one organization, perhaps both.

Rode Hawg kennels' American Bulldog Fujimo Bandit at a lean 98 pounds. Owned by Larry and Karen Kaura in Capron, Illinois.

RIOTS AND CROWD CONTROL

Now here is something that is difficult to train for. It will always be difficult to find volunteers to agitate your dog in any way. It is even more difficult to find large groups of them and to convince them to allow you and your dog to chase them. This segment, I must confess, is almost never going to confront a privately owned protection dog, but the police-dog handler should read this carefully, then re-read it. There are not many things in police work that have the potential of injuring or killing you to the degree that controlling a riot has. I have had a very active career in police work and I've had my share of white-knuckled experiences, including Vietnam. Some of these situations were quite unpleasant, but nothing prepared me for the fear that I would learn in a riot. Remember, courage increases with numbers and is directly proportional to the number of beers consumed. It is easy enough to understand

American Bulldogs Spanky and Kink. Photo by the owner, Sue Miller.

that an officer can feel some apprehension when he has to arrest a really huge guy with no backup. Imagine what goes through his mind when he is facing 1500 drug-and-alcohol-boosted barbarians intent on anarchy and other forms of unacceptable behavior. First let's riot-train the dog as best we can.

Get as many volunteers as possible. Explain to them that the dog will remain on lead throughout the exercise and they won't be in any danger of getting bitten. He will be allowed to get close, but no bites. Believe it or not, this is the best way to handle a real riot too. You don't want any bites because each one is a mountain of paperwork. Also, if your dog locks onto one person he is no longer a threat to the crowd.

It is not uncommon for some idiot to try to grab the dog's tail, ears, neck or collar. This is why a spiked collar is a smart investment. Someone actually did it just recently in Belle Glade, Florida during one of their recent riots. Some rioter grabbed the ear of K-9 Nero and held on in spite of the efforts of Nero and others. Nero will be OK. K-9 Jago pulled a bad guy out from under some sheet metal one night by his ear. The bad guy thought it would be OK to grab Jago by the throat and choke him. It caught Jago by surprise and he didn't know what to do about it for about ten seconds until his handler made a suggestion. I'll never know what the outcome would have been had the handler not made that suggestion. In another incident, the dog was picked up by his collar and bodyslammed seven times. Ample justification for a spiked collar, don't you think? Nick's was two inches wide with three rows of spikes spaced one inch apart. Nobody ever grabbed him. Nobody ever slammed him.

It is also possible that someone in the crowd will get brave and come to the aid of a fallen comrade or family member. Never underestimate the courage of humans. They are unpredictable, but will get into a frenzy over a martyr. Try not to

to do what they perceive as the rescue of their downed friend or family member. Don't let the dog get a bite if possible. The fear of the bite is actually more effective. The fear will make them run and scream. Their running and screaming will panic the rest of the crowd into running and screaming and *that's* what you want. Not a hospital emergency room filled with bleeding martyrs for the news media to interview where they tell the whole world about the police and their killer attack dogs.

Is a badge in the American Bulldog's future? It's possible.

give them one. This is why head shots are forbidden in police baton training. A bleeding head wound doesn't actually do much physical damage, but it bleeds like crazy, giving the impression that it's a mortal wound. Friends of the now bloody rioter decide

In training, let the front two or three rioters wear hidden sleeves and take bites, but make the dog hit and run. This is really a test to see if Fido will herd the rioters or lock on. Locking on is to be discouraged. You may get lucky and have a dog whose

A band of bulldogs search the woods for bad guys.

herding instincts are still strong. He'll do nips instead of bites and get 20 people instead of one. A much better arrangement.

Another thing you don't want is a loose dog. He may only split the crowd and get into big trouble while out of your sight. Nick got past me one night as I was opening his door and ran into the crowd. Only two people out of a crowd of perhaps 300 reported being bitten. At least 20 people were hit by his front feet and muzzle. He put ten men on top of a two-man ice box and six men up a one-man tree. The rest of the crowd was busy screaming and trampling each other. I had a hard time calling him back because of the pandemonium and his tunnel vision. I was lucky. The ideal is to let the dog out to the full 6-foot length of the leash (leather) and let him fan out to both sides of you in a half circle. He should be mostly on his hind legs and showing a lot of teeth. If your decoys are doing a credible job of civil agitation (lots of escalating, argumentative threats and yelling), the dog won't need any encouragement from you.

During the initial phase of agitation it's real easy to teach him a warning command, such as "guard" or "watch." When the aggressor approaches, he is given the command that he should pay attention. Immediately following this command, the aggressor pops him. In very short order he connects the warning with the attack and becomes quite alert. This is important with a green dog or one that sees very little action. He can become complacent just as a man can.

After our first riot I never had to use the watch word again because Nick was streetwise. Even the dumbest dog will get streetwise ten times more quickly than the more intelligent human. I guess it's because they are the more primitive animal of the two and haven't lost their survival instincts to the degree that humans have. This is what makes them such fabulous partners in police work. You may often miss a tell-tale sign that a suspect warrants your closer attention. You may miss the fear in his eyes or his glancing around for an escape route or where his hands are. A streetwise dog won't. The late K-9 Bear of Belle Glade, Florida caught something early in his career that his handler Sgt. Ron Shunk missed. Ron was pulling a guy out of a car when Bear bit the man's hand, apparently for no reason. Ron was not pleased. Until he stepped on the gun that had been in the man's hand. I suspect Ron still misses that mutt.

War Stories

What would a book about police/protection dogs be without a few hairy stories taken from real-life exploits of real police and protection dogs? I'll waste no more time. Enjoy.

ARMED ROBBERY IN PROGRESS

It was 3:34 a.m. when the phone rang. I caught it halfway through the first ring. Nick had been lying asleep at my feet as I watched T.V. He was now very much awake, tail wagging and whining. He knew what the phone call meant. It meant that he and I were going hunting. We were a police K-9 team and manhunting was our job. We trained once a week for it and we were good at it.

I pulled on the side zip combat boots and holstered the black 9 mm. I then held out a 2-inch-wide black leather collar with three rows of spikes at knee level. The dog placed his muzzle between my thighs as I buckled it. By the time I dropped the walky into its holster and put on the ballcap, the dog was making 6-foot leaps straight up. Our adrenaline was starting to flow and he didn't control it as well as I did. We jumped into the K-9 car and, with fingers of blue light flicking off the palm trees lining the road, we headed for the ghetto at 110 mph. The phone call had advised of an armed robbery in progress. I fully expected the competition to be gone when we arrived, but I was also expecting to have to track them on pavement. Scent doesn't stay on pavement very long so speed is of the essence.

On arrival we were told by the officer on the scene that we had missed their departure by about one minute. He advised me about a tee-shirt dropped at the scene by one of the gunmen. It was still lying on the floor in front of the register. The officer had the clerk shut down the all-night "Stop & Rob" and kept pedestrians from entering the parking lot and spoiling the track with their own scent. The dog was introduced to the tee-shirt, which he grabbed and shook. We then left the store on a dead run with Nick's nose about six inches off the pavement. Luckily there was absolutely no breeze to disperse the scent and almost no civilians on the street to get in the way or spoil the track.

We covered about three blocks with Nick pulling so hard that he was leaving white marks on the pavement with his toenails. He suddenly stopped and stood up on his rear legs just a bit. Scent was in the air, which meant the competition was very close. Nick dragged me through a 6-foot-high hedge and into a yard. All his hair was up and he was whining, which meant our guy was probably close enough for *me* to smell. The 9 mm was unholstered and Nick was unhooked. He was frantic because scent was everywhere; the bad guy had been running and was scared to death. He was putting out enough odor that I really could smell him now. I spotted him about two seconds before Nick did. He was sitting under a house with eyes as big as dinner plates watching Nick's every move. He was motionless and Nick wasn't sure it was a bad guy because it wasn't moving. His hands were between his legs, concealed from my view, and I didn't like that. I couldn't see if he was still armed with the double-barreled sawed-off 12-gauge used in the robbery. Nick was staring at him but not attacking because there was still no movement. I wanted Nick all over the guy. We needed movement before Nick would go off, so I slipped up behind him next to the house that he was sitting under. I applied the sole of my boot to the side of the guy's head, while observing him over the sights of my pistol. He started to topple over. Nick exploded onto the bad guy. I saw empty hands come up quickly to protect his face. Nick got a shoulder hold and I got Nick's collar, dragging them both out from under the house. I handcuffed him then outed Nick, who was now furiously wagging his tail and yipping for more. The bad guy quickly ratted out his cronies by name, and we snagged them walking casually down the street ten minutes later. They were still wearing the same clothes they had done the robbery in. We turned them over to the on-duty officer, went home and turned in. I didn't fall asleep till about noon because of the adrenaline rush. At about 2 p.m. I woke up because Nick was barking and running in his sleep. I guess adrenaline was still in his system too.

BURGLARS' BREAKFAST OF CHAMPIONS

At 2:13 a.m. a citizen came into the police station. He had just driven past the Dollar General store and saw three men messing with the paper machines in front of the store. It was his assumption, and

mine, that they were trying to remove the money. The only other patrol unit arrived just ahead of me. We got out and checked all the machines. They were all fine and no one was in the area. The other car had already left and I was about to, when I caught movement out of the corner of my eye. When I looked at the storefront, I saw a man's head and shoulders disappear from the doorway. He was on his hands and knees. For a split second I thought he must be part of a cleanup crew. Then I thought otherwise. He was part of a cleanup crew all right, except the eight garbage bags ready to go out the front door were filled with everything but garbage. I parked my K-9 car in front of the supermarket next door and walked back to where I had seen the man.

I noticed the glass in the door was plexiglass. It was intact and in place, but when pushed it went in at the bottom where the retaining frame had been kicked off. The frame was lying about six feet away on the floor. I radioed my partner and requested he arrive quietly at the rear door with no lights. At the same time the dispatcher was on the phone getting additional backup from the county. My partner joined me at the front, assuring me there were no rear windows and that the door wouldn't open because his police car was parked against it. Nick had known all along that something was up and was already in the front seat with his head out the window, eagerly awaiting the hand signal to come. A quiet horizontal flick of my left hand brought Nick out the window and to my left side. We were both really keyed up because this was to be our first real business burglary (in progress) in the three years that we were active. Not that we were in a crime-free town. Far from it! Business burglary simply came to a screeching halt the day Nick hit the street. An occasional smash and grab would happen but no burglaries. I took a lot of pride in that but I sure wanted to nail one inside. We trained for three years just for this night! Holding Nick by his spiked collar I pulled back the plexiglass and yelled an unmistakable warning to come out or be dog-bitten. No answer and frankly, I didn't want one. I just wanted to let them know we were coming. This way, they'd have time to imagine the worst. What I really wanted was to scare the hell out of them. You see, when you're scared, *really* scared, your heart starts pounding. You hyperventilate. You sweat and the adrenal glands go into red alert.

A dog can smell adrenaline. You may have heard that dogs can sense that you're scared? True. They smell the adrenaline. This makes it so easy for the dog to find you, it's almost criminal. It is also my opinion that two or three minutes of stark raving terror will go a long way toward providing the necessary incentive to make a burglar think twice before plying his trade in my town. A few good hard bites reinforces it and leaves an impression on the old memory bank as well as the anatomy.

Nick and I entered the store. I growled the command, "find!" He was off. In about 13 seconds Nick was alerting to something on the floor. I paralleled him from 30 feet away and saw the man first because I was taller than Nick and the slacks racks that our man was trying to use for cover. Nick was going around the racks and had the bad guy's full attention. He had been in a crouch but now as Nick

was closing on him he dropped onto his back so he could mulekick the dog. He was unaware that I was coming from behind. As he drew his legs up to smash Nick's face, I aimed a blow at his collar bone just like they teach in the police academy. As luck would have it, I missed the collar bone and put one upside his head—unintentionally, of course. It made a sound very similar to a home run and our perpetrator, who was on his back, spun a little so that when he kicked, it missed Nick by a 12-inch margin. Being unamused by the effort, Nick seized the day and a leg. When the festivities were over and the competition was handcuffed, his efforts to kick were null and void because Nick had pulled his pants down around his ankles. When our citizen of the month demanded that I help him up, I grabbed a double handful of hair and assisted the man to his feet. He was outraged at my refusal to pull up his pants and fasten them. Nick was outraged at his outrage and lunged for his crotch. Not to worry. I was holding his collar.

I told the guy I couldn't hold the dog and pull his pants up at the same time, which did he want me to do? He stated that holding the dog seemed like the best idea to him. He then followed my next suggestion and hopped out of the store with his pants around his ankles. I radioed the backup units that he was coming out and that I would continue the search for additional burglars. As Nick and I went deeper into the store we heard the cops busting a gut when our tough guy hopped through the door and into the headlights of the patrol cars. We cleared the front of the store and entered the rear storage and office area. In about ten seconds

Nick was climbing a wall in the office. Of course no one was there, but I had learned that Nick never lied. The reason he was alerting on the wall was because scent was coming down the wall from the ceiling above. Sure enough, when we exited the office I saw a loft above the office with about 50 large cardboard boxes in it. We made our way into the loft by climbing boxes next to it. The loft had no guardrail, so I took Nick up on lead. He started tearing into the boxes with a vengeance. When I shoved the last one aside I was pointing my pistol into the face of a very unhappy camper. He never saw the pistol, only the dog straining to get at him. He quickly agreed to follow us down out of the loft and then to my delight, attempted to run out of the building. He made less than 20 feet. A hard full-mouth bite drove home the point, or points as it were. He was cuffed and sent out the door to the waiting officers. Nick and I returned to the search, and I knew where Nick would be alerting next. The second loft above the employee bathroom was where Nick was looking and barking. He was called to a heel and I announced that anyone in the loft should come down or get bitten. The guy surrendered quickly. He didn't try to run, much to.the disappointment of the backup units who were pressing their noses against the windows in hopes of seeing Nick win another one. Oh, well. Two out of three is acceptable.

IT WAS LIKE A SCENE FROM "SMOKEY"

At least that's what the headline said the day after one of our stranger and certainly most publicized adventures. Nick and I were minding our own business patrolling the city one night when I saw a familiar face inside the same old "Stop & Rob." I knew there were outstanding warrants for this guy's arrest for failure to pay child support. He was a middle-aged guy and pretty quiet. He ran his own pool hall and generally stayed out of trouble (when his wife wasn't shooting him). When he exited the store, I quietly told him about the warrants and gave him the choice of riding with me or following me to the station in his car. He said he would follow. He really should have, but no. He and his girlfriend got in her Chevette and he made a run for it. I couldn't believe he was running from a misdemeanor warrant, but here we went.

I radioed the station and let them know I was "in pursuit." He blew through a congested intersection where 300-500 people normally were in the middle of the street. He did the intersection at about 60. I did it at 70. People were literally diving over the hoods of parked cars. After about six blocks he made a left. As I made the left I watched him jump from the still-rolling car and run toward the alley. I tried to lightly thump him with the fender of my car but missed him by a hair. Jamming on the brake, I jumped from the car yelling "Nick Come," which had the same effect Supercalafragilisticexpialidocious usually has on him.

That's right, Nick looked at me like I had two heads! I'm thinking, great! Here I am running through a pedestrian alley that more resembles an obstacle course because of all the garbage cans, mops, tricycles, strollers, rocking chairs, broken TVs and shopping carts, chasing a guy in the rain and of course I haven't even taken the time to grab a flashlight or nightstick. It's the darkest night in written history and most of the street lights have been shot out and my idiot dog is still in the car afraid he might get his feet wet and ruin his pedicure! One could surmise I was less than pleased.

The guy finally clotheslined himself and went down with a thud. I helped him up and said something clever like "you're under arrest" and grabbed a wrist attempting to cuff him. We were both wet now and he was real slippery. He wiggled free and pushed me against a house trailer. It was so dark I could hardly see him but when he pushed me, he stumbled back a couple of feet and apparently (I thought) into somebody's chained-up watchdog. I could hear the dog growling and shaking the guy and the guy screaming just about the way you would expect a guy to scream with someone's dog clamped onto his butt. I couldn't see the dog at all. He was behind the guy in a shadow. I wasn't about to get bitten rescuing the guy so I just figured I'd get my guy whenever the dog got tired of him. In the meantime I'm yelling encouragement to this citizen hero dog like, "Good boy!, Git him!, Eat him up!" After a little time, man and dog emerged from out of the shadow of the house and imagine my surprise when I saw my dog clamped onto the south end of my northbound absconder. I thanked Nick for squeezing me into his busy schedule and finally joining the festivities. I outed the dog and started to cuff our prisoner. He pushed me again and I went into an open septic tank.

Nick the wonder dog made him pay dearly for it but it was too late. As I extricated Mom's favorite boy from the magma, my puppy was busy tearing the pants off the bad guy. By the time I attained a standing posture, Nick had the pants and underwear completely off him and was shaking them vigorously. Unfortunately while he did this, our bad guy was making good his escape although naked from the waist down. I called him off the pants and sent him after the man. Nick caught him by the butt again in the next block. Backup had arrived by now and Dennis and I ran across the street to join Nick and friend. One might think I had learned my lesson by now, but no. I again outed the dog before handcuffing the man. Again, he fought. Again, Nick countered. Again, I outed him before cuffing him. Again, he fought. Again Nick came in but this time he scared the hell out of all of us. He went right for the guy's crotch! I only *thought* I'd heard that guy screaming before. Now he was really screaming and drawing a crowd.

In the heat of the action, the now very excited bad guy was screaming about his worst fear and his bitten body part. I was having a quiet heart attack and expecting the crowd to get ugly and make a riot out of it. As I again tried to cuff him he struggled and Dennis took a punch in the eye. Nick got an ankle. I outed him and the naked, bleeding man ran towards the crowd. I gave chase holding Nick's collar (because of the crowd). I got his shirttail as he entered his mother's trailer and slammed the door, leaving me standing in the rain looking like a fool. Not knowing if he had weapons in the trailer, we stayed out and called for more backup. Once dressed he calmed down and gave up without further incident.

He was treated for the bites at the emergency room and released. That very special bite only turned out to be a pinch. It seems he was a chubby guy with thighs that rubbed together at the top. Nick's lower canines got hung up in his thighs and his top canines sunk into the fat covering his groin area. If the man had been slimmer, it could have been a lot worse.

The lesson I learned that night was once the dog is on the man, *leave him on the man until the man is handcuffed.* If I had done that, I would never have done my now famous half gainer into a septic tank. The man would never have been stripped and bitten in front of 50 hostile witnesses and I wouldn't have been worried about him showing off 20 puncture marks to a grand jury instead of four.

When I first got into K-9, I thought it might appear gruesome to passersby to see the dog chewing on what appeared to be a downed and helpless man while the officer slowly and casually handcuffed him so as to allow the dog all the fun possible. In training we always got the dogs off the decoy as soon as possible and we never cuffed them because of the sleeve, but then they never resumed fighting once the dog was outed. That was training. In the real world, the accosted do resume fighting when they are able. So make sure they are not able. Cuff them *before* outing the dog.

If your dog is really hyped, he might be tugging or even dragging the offender. If your dog is tugging or dragging the man and you are afraid of causing a gruesome spectacle, sit on the guy while you cuff him. This will prevent the dog from dragging him and shocking the finer sensibilities of the aristocrats driving by in their limo with their videocamera rolling. There will be only four puncture marks instead of 20. Think about it.

THE INFAMOUS CHRISTMAS NIGHT MASSACRE

It was 11:29 p.m. when I turned west onto what was commonly known as Wash House Street. This wasn't the correct name of the street but was due to its having the only laundromat in the ghetto. There were exactly 31 minutes left in this Christmas Day, and I guess the locals were grabbing all the gusto they could.

The one and only business establishment that was open on this holy night was, you guessed it, a bar. A bar where alcohol was served to anyone tall enough to put the money on the bar. A bar where one could also score any and all kinds of drugs, and score it they did! I can only estimate the number of revelers at perhaps 1500. That's ten times the normal amount of people in the area on any Saturday night, an area that would be considered crowded with 50 people. Another estimate is that 60% of them were drunk,. 70% were on drugs and virtually 100% of them were in a state of high anxiety, bordering on mayhem. I guessed there must be a fight going on in the grassy lot between the laundromat and the bar because people were trampling each other to get closer to it. I couldn't actually see the combatants through the crowd (they may have been on the ground). A thought crossed my mind that it might be wise to just keep driving since no one had actually called the police yet and I was the only officer on duty. When I had come on duty the dispatcher asked if she should call the other officer and see what was keeping him. He was normally punctual, so I figured he'd be along in a few minutes and told her to skip the call. I would learn later that he was sound asleep in bed.

I just about had my mind made up to put the car in reverse and get the hell out of there anyway. I should have, but then hindsight is always 20/20, isn't it? Right at this critical moment of decision, Barbara called me on the radio and said, "I think there's a fight on Wash House Street" I told her I thought she was right, and I would need backup (a flame thrower and a miracle is what I really needed). I parked the K-9 car and hooked Nick up to a six-foot leash, the theory being that no one can get within six feet of you. Yeah, right. I attempted to bring Nick through the crowd but every time I tried, an idiot would run by screaming and Nick would lunge for them. Not wanting him to lock on to a non-combatant, I had to hold him short, which compromised his effectiveness. While I was figuring out what I should try next, a powerfully built young deputy arrived and calmly inquired as to whether his assistance would be needed. His name was Jim Dickinson. I answered in the affirmative.

Just then another idiot walked up to us in an obviously agitated state. He had been in part of the fight and looked it. He made the grandiose announcement that we needed to lock him up because he intended to kill someone. That seemed like a reasonable request to me in light of the guy's current emotional state and his past emotional state, with which I was thoroughly familiar.

This guy was a professional pain in the butt. I had no doubt that he probably started the fight and deserved whatever he got for the effort. I told him he was under arrest and to start moving toward my car. He then boldly announced that there "wasn't no cop could put

him in no car." That brought a smile to Jim's face. I handed him my cuffs and firmed up my grip on Nick's leash. When Jim got a wrist in a vise-like grip, the guy balled up a fist and raised it. Nick didn't wait for a command. He rushed right in and I gave him the required slack in the leash. One sixteenth of an inch short of a K-9 vasectomy, I stopped my dog but kept him right there snapping at the man's crotch. It always amazes me what a tranquilizing effect that has on even the most determined berserkers. He relaxed the balled-up fist as his violent, combative resistance turned to passive compliance by a four-legged police dynamo that barely weighed 70 pounds. Jim stuffed him in the back seat of my car for me. We were about to leave when a beer bottle whistled past my head, breaking on the windshield of my car. Jim and I both saw who did it and not only was he not running but he was reloading his right hand from a half dozen more cradled in his left arm. I said to Jim, "We're going to put him in jail no matter what it takes." Jim said, "You got that right." We ran over to him and Jim put two-and-one-half inches of stainless steel gun barrel up his nose, while Nick was snapping close enough to his crotch that his stainless steel caps were making sparks on the guy's zipper. This man was quite happy to be cuffed by Jim and led away from the now frothing Nick. Jim and I agreed that right about now would be an excellent time to break camp and head for more pleasant surroundings. Jim's car was 50 yards away and I waited until he was in it before Nick and I loaded up.

About the time I shut the door, rocks and bottles started to hit the car. Then a brick came through the right rear glass. It exploded, sending fragments into the face of the man who was sitting on that side of the back seat. Another brick came through the window, followed by a barrage of bricks, rocks, bottles, and I think concrete blocks because the impact of the missiles was actually rocking the car now. I was afraid the next brick would come through a front window and would kill either me or my dog. Being at a temporary loss to remember any of my college psychology, I got out of the car, drawing a 44 magnum, and fired a shot into the air. I then aimed into the crowd, determined to make a respectable last stand. To my amazement they were scattering. It looked like Moses parting the Red Sea. Not one to argue with success or belabor a point, I put the car in drive and burned rubber. After making about 50 feet I heard an old man yelling, "Hey man, you forgot your dog!"

Now I was really getting angry. If one hair on that dog's head was harmed I would have called for an air strike. Jamming on the brakes, I slid to a stop and as the door opened a familiar cold nose nudged my left arm. I reached out, grabbed Nick by the skin on his back, slung him across my lap and smoked the tires once more. The wind quickly shut the open door for me, saving me a little time. I yelled a somewhat profane request for backup units into the radio mike. I made another right turn to see if Jim had escaped intact. He had and was heading for my station at warp speed.

He and I were close after that. He was intelligent, warm, funny and friendly and loved being a cop. Who would have guessed that five years after surviving the Christmas Night

Massacre and pulling my fat out of the fire, Jim Dickinson would be murdered by a chronic alcoholic with a rifle? When they pull the switch on that guy, they can charge it to my electric bill. About two weeks before his death, I spoke with Jim while we gassed up our patrol cars. We laughed and joked about the massacre. Goodbye Jim.

PRISON BREAK!

A dog named Bear was a skinny German Shepherd K-9 who really got things going in the Lake Okeechobee area of South Florida around 1978 or so. There is a state prison just outside the Belle Glade city limits. It is famous not for who it confined, but because of who escaped. Virtually everybody! I always stifled a desire to write a letter to the warden and suggest that they install locks on the cell doors. Anyway, during what seemed like the weekly prison break, the state people couldn't get their dogs to track or something, I don't know what, so they called out Ron Shunk and his dog Bear from the Belle Glade P.D. Perhaps some of the details were forgotten but the gist of it was that Ron was shown where the man was last seen. He started Bear on the track and all was going well. As I remember it, Bear covered a lot of ground before wading into a stream. Ron followed until Bear stopped midstream and started barking. Absolutely no one was around. Ron thought Bear was losing it. He put him back on lead and took him back to the starting point and told him to track. Bear put his nose to the ground, retraced his own footsteps and led Ron back to the same stream. He waded into the middle and began barking again. Ron was quite disgusted with him and started over one more time. Another repeat performance convinced Ron that he needed a new dog. He went home in disgust. Later (I think the next morning) the convict was found walking down the road and was brought back to the booking room at the Belle Glade jail. Ron couldn't stand the curiosity. He drove over to the jail where the convict was being processed and asked him how he had managed to evade his dog. He told Ron that every time Bear stopped in the stream, the dog had been standing on his chest! He had been lying on his back in the stream, breathing through a reed.

I wasn't there, but I believe it to be the truth. Another book could be written about Bear because he had a very long career in a very busy town, but Ron will have to write that one.

THE RIGHT DOG IN THE RIGHT PLACE

Years ago I was having a training problem with a Rottweiler and wanted a second opinion from a trainer who had lots of experience with the breed. That's how I met Jeff Leonard and Norm Garner. After they evaluated the dog, we got down to serious conversation about dogs, women, sports, war, politics and back to dogs. They did protection training on all kinds of dogs. One of the dogs that caught my eye was a Pit Bull who was there for OB training. He was gorgeous. Solid red with a black nose. He was happy, alert, friendly and all muscle. I was petting him through the fence and pipe dreaming out loud to Jeff and Norm, saying, "Wouldn't it be great to have one of these for a police dog?" Jeff said he preferred the German Shepherd, but admitted Pit Bulls were great dogs. He added that they had a bad reputation due mainly to their appetite for other dogs. Because of this, they could only be used for personal protection, but they were exceptional in that line of work. He then smiled and said, "Ask Norm." Norm was quiet and staring at the horizon. After a long silence, I said, "Well?" He shrugged and told me that he once owned a female Pit Bull named Blaze. He and Jeff trained her all the way and she became Norm's housedog. He had been married at the time and they were expecting a child. Norm was gone somewhere when a guy came to the door. Norm's wife didn't know him and wouldn't let him in even though he told her Norm knew him and said it would be OK. It was a flimsy door and was easily forced open. He walked in with a big smile. When he reached for her, he got a faceful of Pit Bull, or more accurately the Pit Bull got a mouthful of face. After a minute of fighting and screaming (from everyone), the guy got smart and either passed out or pretended to. The dog released him and went over to her mistress, sat down and quietly watched the man on the floor. Norm's wife was totally hysterical and just continued to scream and cry.

Ready? The guy got up and came across the room like Frankenstein with a bloody face, wearing a very crooked smile, and attempted to grab the wife again, totally ignoring the dog! Well, the dog didn't ignore him. When Norm returned and ran through the mangled door, he found his hysterical wife huddled in a corner and his dog still attached to the monster's face. On verbal command she outed and came to a heel at Norm's side, tail wagging. To the disappointment of all, the man lived.

Norm's wife divorced him because of the incident. Apparently the violence of the incident really had a psychologically damaging effect on her. She chose to shun the dog that saved her and her unborn child and divorce the man who trained it.

The guy's face required all the king's horses and all the king's men to put the mangled mess together again. I forget all the grisly details, but the left cheekbone went for sure. That's not really unusual. Any hard biter can do that kind of damage. Facial bones are rather delicate. After being knocked through the ropes several times, Jack Dempsey climbed back into the ring and broke nearly every bone in Jess Willard's face, and he was wearing padded gloves!

So are you getting the idea that a dog can do a lot of damage? Are you getting the idea that under certain circumstances, a dog could even cause the death of a human being? Does that scare you? If you answered yes to all three questions, you are intelligent, mature, responsible and probably capable of owning and caring for a protection-trained dog.

Are you under the impression that attack training and protection training are pretty much the same thing? If you answered yes, you are wrong. Here's why. Attack-trained is a term coined by the military to describe a certain type of sentry dog confined to a certain area for the purpose of keeping intruders out. This type of dog is trained to attack anyone in his perimeter. Anyone. He works without a handler most of the time. He is purposely not socialized because he is to be as antisocial as possible. He is perfect for missile bases and bomb dumps or any other area requiring a high level of security. He is totally useless outside of this type of environment because he's just too nasty for the civilized world.

If you have a dog trained with the methods discussed in this book, you have a protection-trained dog, not an attack-trained dog. The important difference is that the protection dog is controllable. He will out on command. The attack dog works without a handler, hence—no control, no out. Point? Simple: you want a man–stopper to protect your home and family. You don't want a man–killer in that role. You couldn't afford the liability insurance for him. There is a videotape available for rent called *Faces of Death*. It has three parts to it. I don't recall which tape, but one of them shows a man being killed by two attack dogs in a junkyard. It's quite sobering. A protection dog, on the other hand, can go with the family anywhere. He's controllable in any situation because of his extensive socialization, and he comes on only when reacting to the aggressive human.

So if anyone asks you (especially plaintiff's council) if your dog is attack-trained, by all means say no! Remember, if you're being sued because Rosco bit someone, the opposing council will eventually get around to painting the picture for the jury that your dog is an uncontrollable monster that lives to bite innocent people like Norm's house guest, and that you are both culpable and negligent by not keeping the dog secured in a steel cage surrounded by a moat. Anyone intelligent enough to be reading this book doesn't need to be apprised of the ridiculous lawsuits that some people will attempt to get rich on. Don't be the next victim of one of these clowns. Keeping the dog on a chain could accomplish this.

When people who ask me the question, "Why do you keep a watchdog in your house instead of on a chain in the yard?" I tell them that everything that I love and value is in the house. If my dog is on a chain the only thing he can protect is a circle of bare dirt within the chain.

What I'm trying to say is don't even start to train the dog if he's not going to live in the house with you. If that is your plan, then you've wasted your money buying this book. You can't do that and expect him to be a deterrent. Can you imagine how things might have turned out if Norm had his dog on a chain?

The same dog broke the latch on a pop-out rear car window and saved Norm a thorough thrashing one night. He was attacked by a guy and was doing such a good job of defending himself that several of the guy's friends came running to assist him. Blaze didn't much care for that and bailed out of Norm's Pinto. She tore into a few and the fight was over. She and Norm were allowed to leave without further interference. Norm is still a professional trainer and is attending a police academy in the southeastern part of the U.S. When I recently asked what his preference was for a police or protection dog, his answer was a bit of a surprise. He stated he had no preference as long as they have the right stuff. He does agree, however, that Pit Bulls and American Bulldogs possess the right stuff to a high degree. His current personal dog is a 40-pound Malinois. I've heard from people who know the dog that he is a four-legged phenomenon. I don't doubt it. Norm calls him his undercover dog because no one would ever take him for what he is and he can be concealed under Norm's coat. Interesting concept, I thought.

Conditioning the Working Dog

Owned and trained by Al Banuelos, Banuelos' Predator SchHII—80 lbs. in shape.

The working dog needs to maintain a lean body weight and muscles that are ready to go. If his job is accomplishing feats of derring-do, he'd better not be carrying excess baggage or his energy level will be disappointingly low. This is probably why we don't see too many fat guys playing basketball.

A once-a-week training schedule is good for keeping his skills sharp, but falls short of keeping him hard and lean. Roadwork is the answer, but can be hard on the handler. Of course in this day and age of physical fitness, you shouldn't cringe at the thought of jogging with the dog. As long as we know you won't be jogging alongside him, I guess I might as well tell you a few methods of giving *him* a workout. There are actually four ways of running him that I'm aware of without getting you all sweaty.

1. A *bicycle* can give him all the workout he can handle without killing his out-of-shape handler.

2. *Treadmills* made especially for dogs are surprisingly affordable. They are adjustable and can be used in any weather.

3. *Motor vehicles* are good ways of running him. Cars; all-terrain vehicles; trucks. Run him next to it, not behind it. Why, you ask? Ever hear the joke about the old man who bought the mule? Well, it seems he tied it to the back of his big flatbed farm truck and started home. At his arrival home, his wife walked out to meet him in the yard. This was unusual, he said. Yes, she said, but I just had to find out why you're dragging ten pounds of raw meat around the yard...

4. *Swimming* is a terrific workout. It is an exercise that can't overdo or sprain anything. In fact, vets recommend it for sprains on dogs and horses. The best thoroughbred horse farms have special tanks built for swimming their horses on a regular basis. Swimming conditions all the muscles at the same time as well as the cardiovascular system. The simplest way is to toss a floatable toy out into a lake or pool and have him retrieve it. The ocean is a little better if you have one at your disposal.

Sit in a rowboat and have him swim after you. This could work if you kept a wary eye on him and a length of rope on his nylon collar, so as to be able to reel him in when he's tired. An old trick used by dogfighters to condition their dogs is to put them in a nylon harness and attach a rope to it. Find an empty boat slip at a marina. String another rope across the slip, then toss the free rope over it in the center. Attach the dog to the end of the hanging rope and let him swim in one spot. The incentive for Pit Bulls to swim faster is another dog in a crate on the dock right in front of the swimmer. Dogs other than Pit Bulls won't fall for that so the handler can stand in front of him giving verbal encouragement. A toy might also work. Like the mule joke, don't walk away while he's doing his swim.

At least one of these methods should be used on your dog, especially if he's going to be competing in K-9 trials or Schutzhund. Keeping him physically fit will prolong his life and his career. I once saw an Air Force dog (Shepherd) competing at a K-9 trial who was no less than 11 years old! He was in top shape and ready to go. His teeth were worn flat, but it just made him bite harder to hold on to the sleeve. He held on real good.

Don't forget Frisbees® and Plaque Attacker™ from Nylabone®. They both can increase his prey drive. The latter is virtually indestructible and heavy as it is constructed of solid nylon. Rawhide chews get disgusting in a hurry and the first time you step on one in your bare feet, you'll think a Plaque Attacker™ is the better idea. Remember, puppies have to chew and may continue chewing into adulthood, like my Bulldog. I buy cow hooves at the local pet shop. She loves them, and will leave the furniture alone if she's got a couple to chew. She also plays with them. They eat them just like rawhide but can't gag or puke from it like they can from rawhide.

INDEX

Page numbers in **boldface** refer to illustrations.

Books by T.F.H.

H-1063 288 pgs.

TS-143 288 pgs.
Over 250 full
color photos.

TS-141 300 pgs. Over
300 full color photos
and drawings.

H-1069 288 pgs.

H-1024 350 pgs.
65 color photos.

TS-142 320 pgs.
Over 350 color
photos.

KW-221 192 pgs. Over
175 full-color
illustrations.

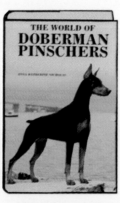

H-1082 640 pgs. Over
800 full color photos
600 B&W photos.

TS-147 448 pgs. Nearly
700 color photos.